YONI BAKER
HERACLES

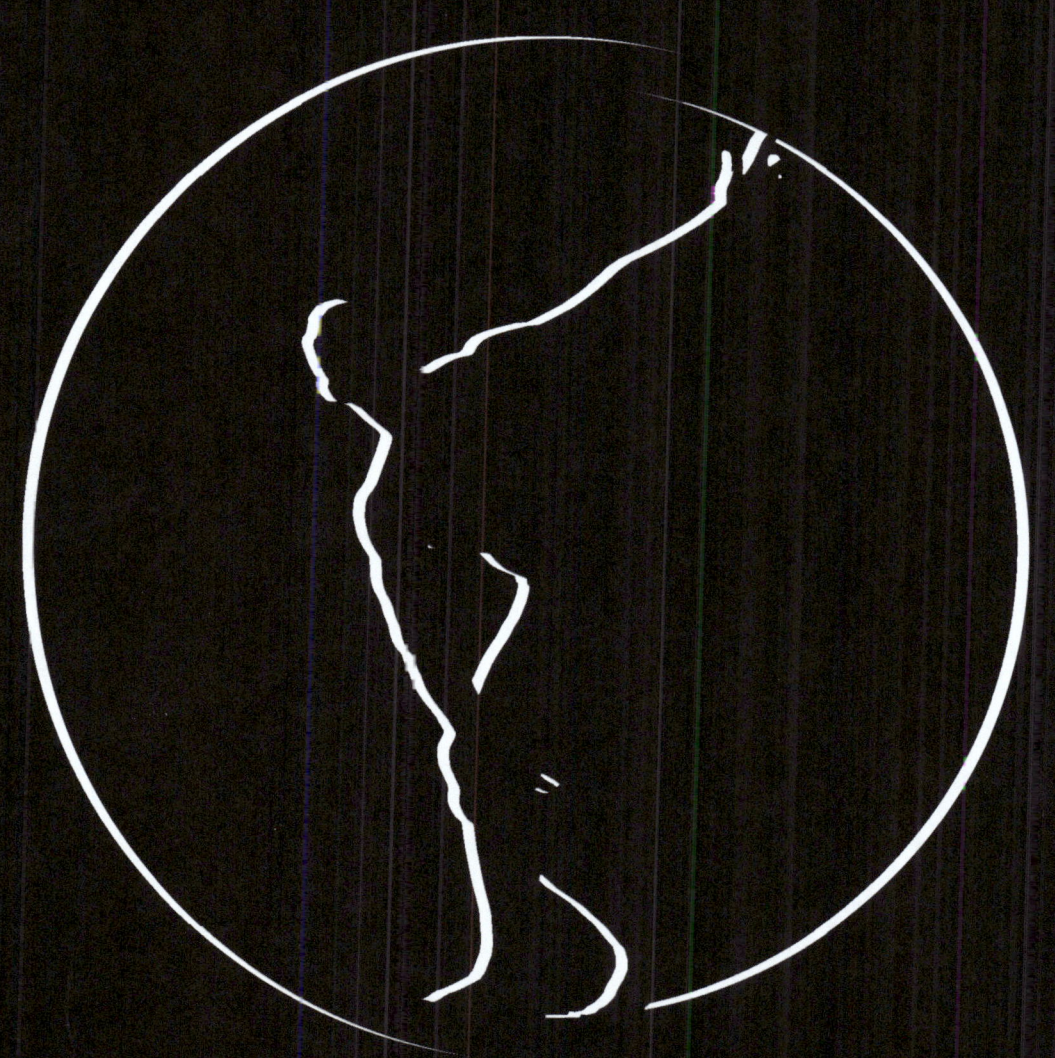

BakerM⊙del

Model: Yoni Baker
www.bakermodel.com

Photographer: Balm in Gilead Photography
Photo retouch: Christa Maier
www.thereisbalmingilead.com

Designer/editor: Brent J. Trembath
www.scruffypuppies.com

© Copyright 2018 Yoni Baker, All rights reserved. No part of this publication may be reproduced, or transmitted in any form or by any means, electronic, mechanical, photocopying, recording, or otherwise, without express permission in writing from Yoni Baker.

FOREWARD

Like my Abba (father in Hebrew) I was born in South Africa. My mom however, was born in Israel. Having a mixed cultural background has provided me with perspective and experience, and having parents that are classically trained artists, names like Picasso, Michelangelo, Bernini, Van Gogh were tossed around in our house the way celebrities were in the houses of my friends.

It was because of my artistic background that led me to sculpting. Inspired by sci-fi, horror, fantasy and our "film crew" in high school, I was led into special effects makeup, where 20 seasons later you can still catch me in the makeup room at the Haunted Hotel in San Diego.

Thanks to my dad, who insisted I watch the first Terminator with Arnold Schwarzenegger all those years ago, I was again inspired by action films. Combined with tennis and swim, I had a new desire in the gym and bodybuilding.

As a fan of super heroes, I remember I used to ride my bike with by friend Phil each week and annoy the comic store clerk behind that huge raised desk by paying with loose change.

As a model I realize that I am a part of something momentary and special, something that lies beneath the surface, creative and full of dimension and soul. Being on stage, I tell a story of my character. Sadness, remorse, happiness, love, wisdom… I want to push the abilities of the artist and give of myself to better their skills.

Years ago, my mom modeled for the Arts Students League in New York. Speaking with her on the subject, she mentioned that she did a lot of warrior poses. My eyebrow lifted, "me too mom, me too."

- Yoni

Please feel free to tag me with your creations on social media !

@bakermodel

www.facebook.com/yonimodel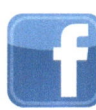

Or search Baker Model on Facebook

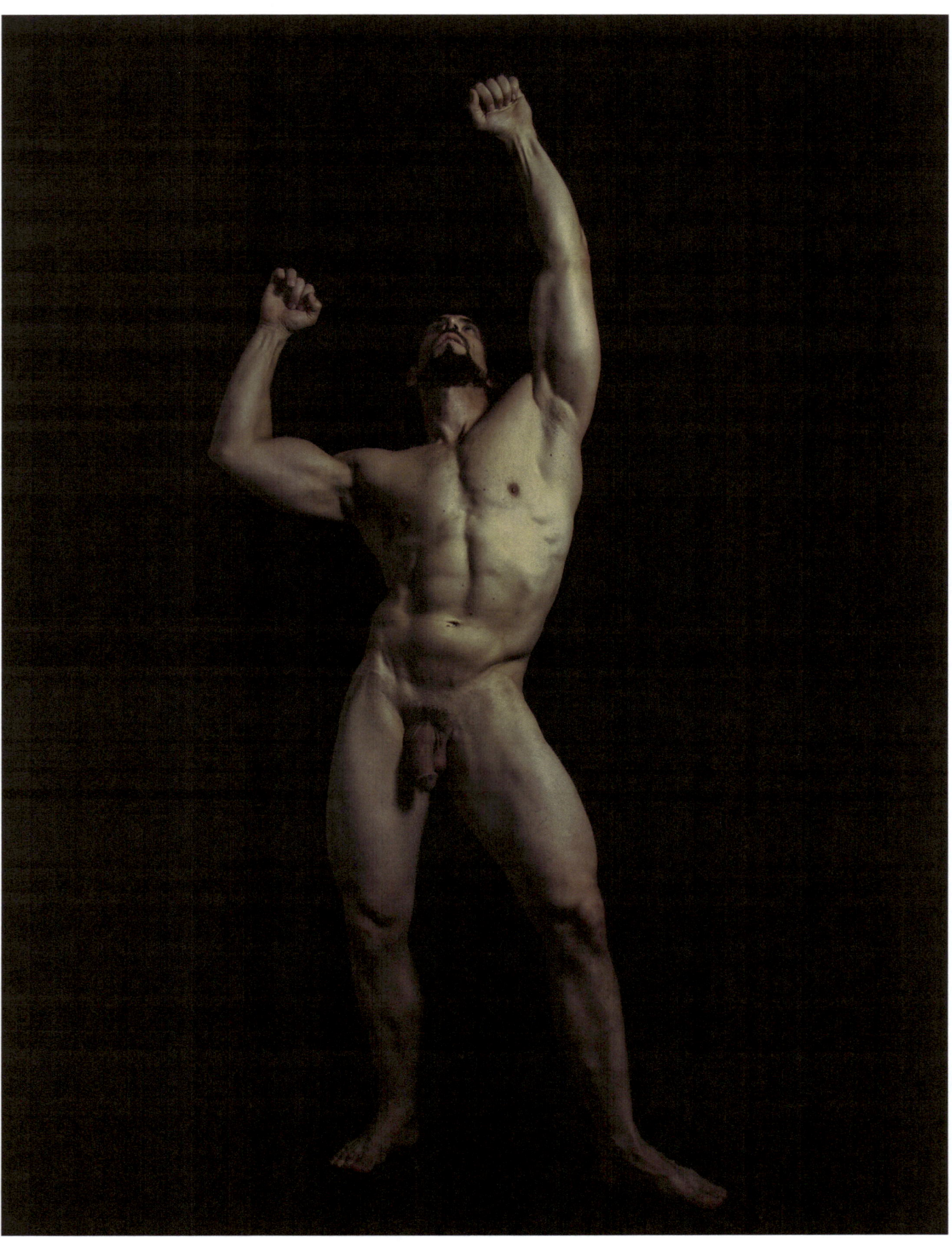

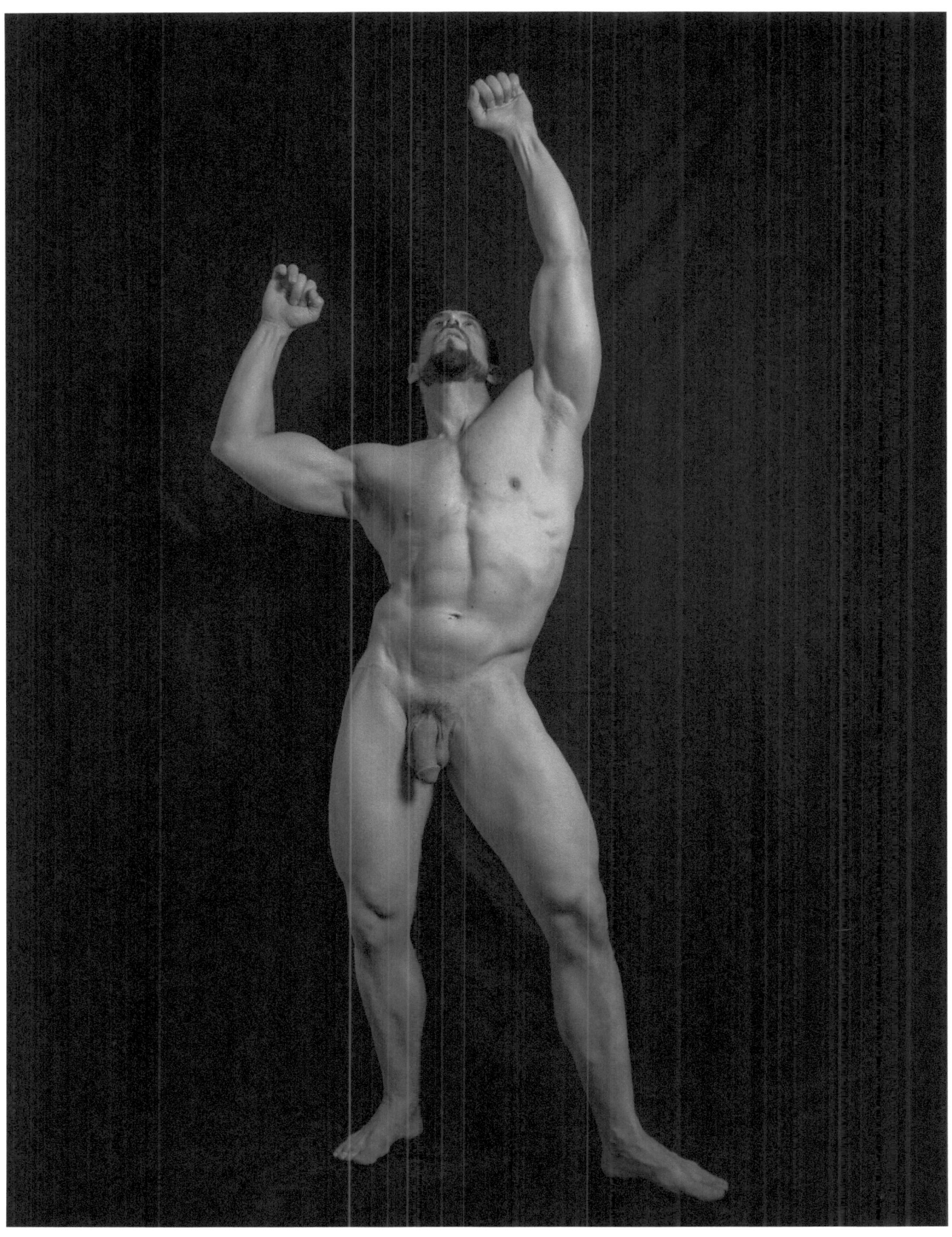

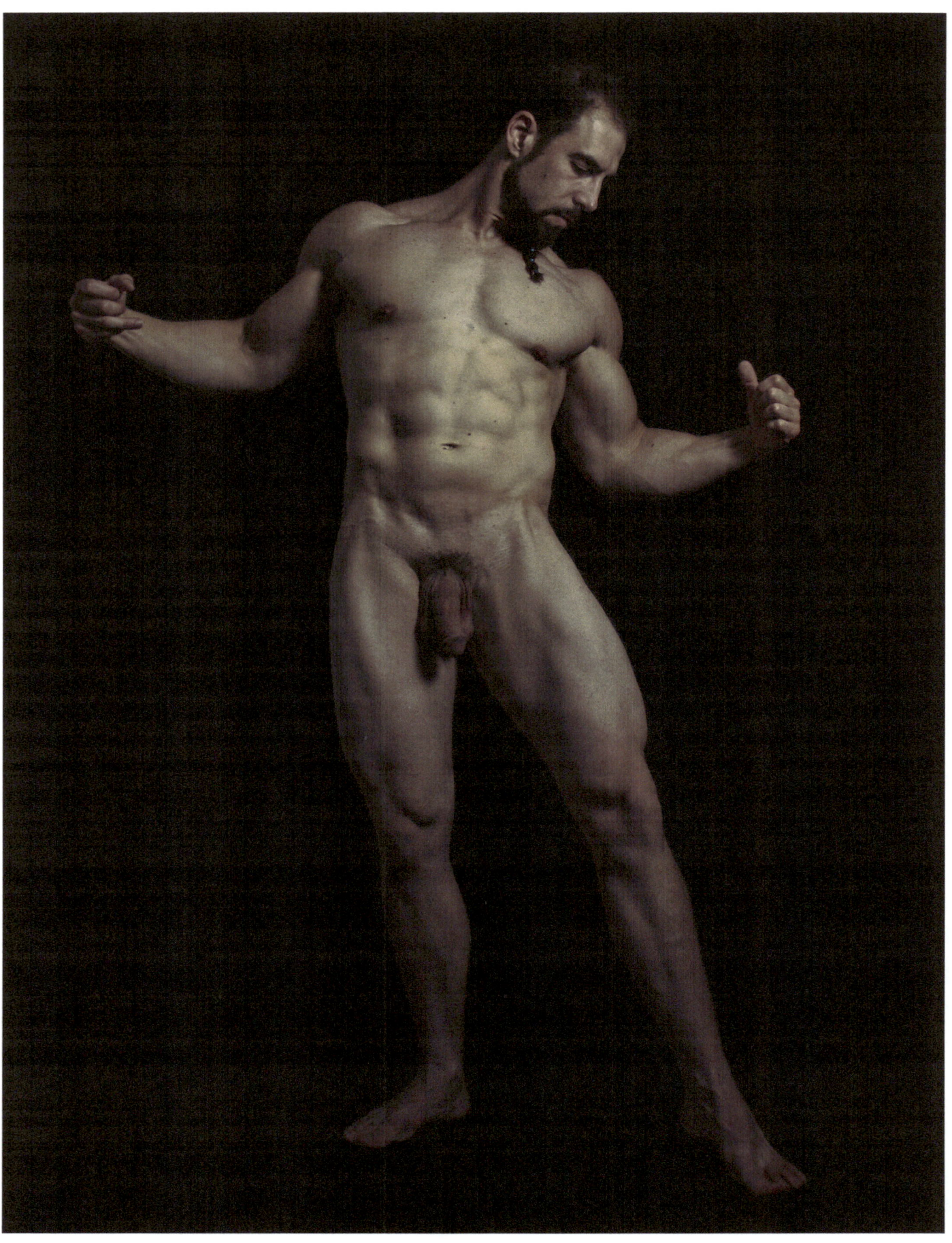

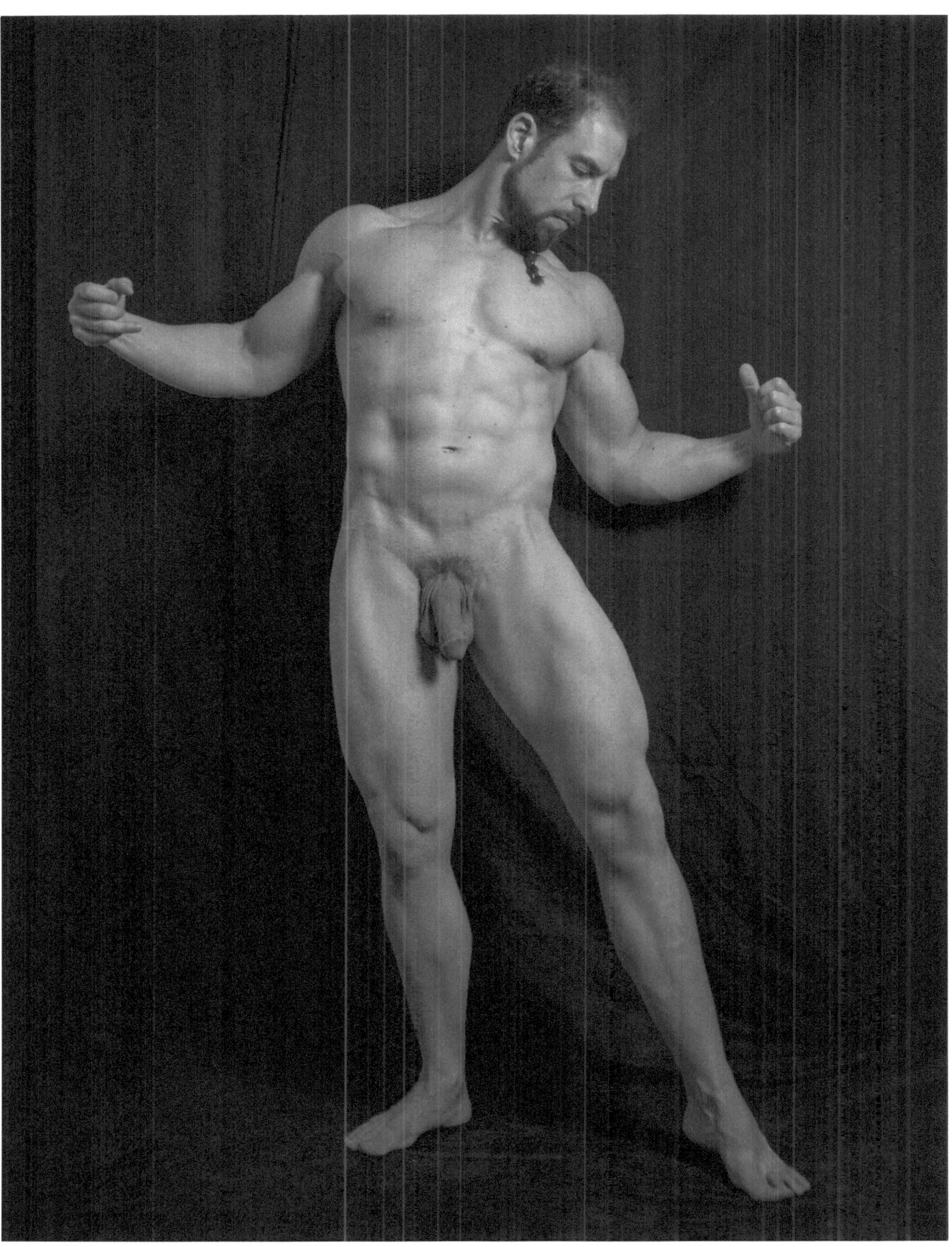

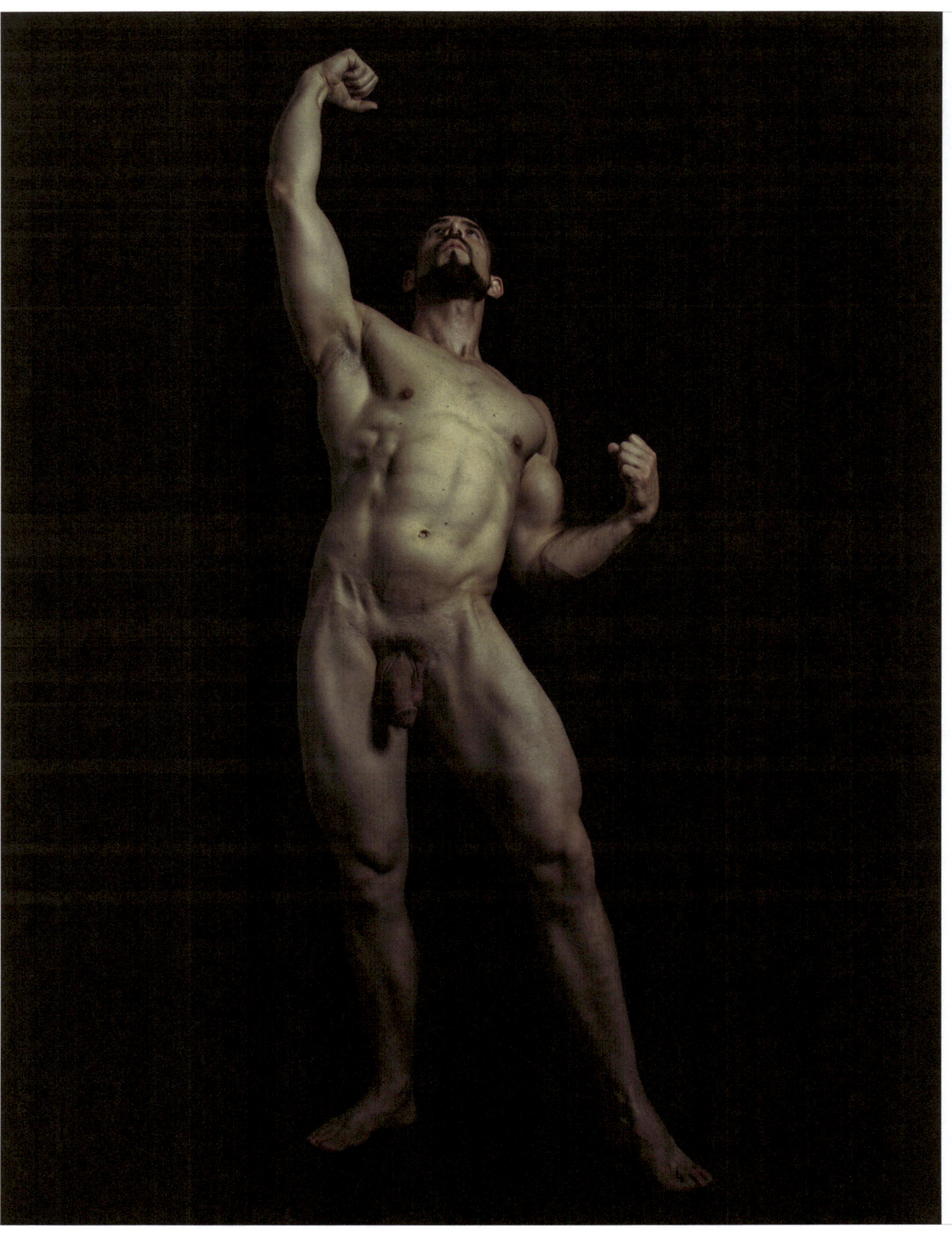

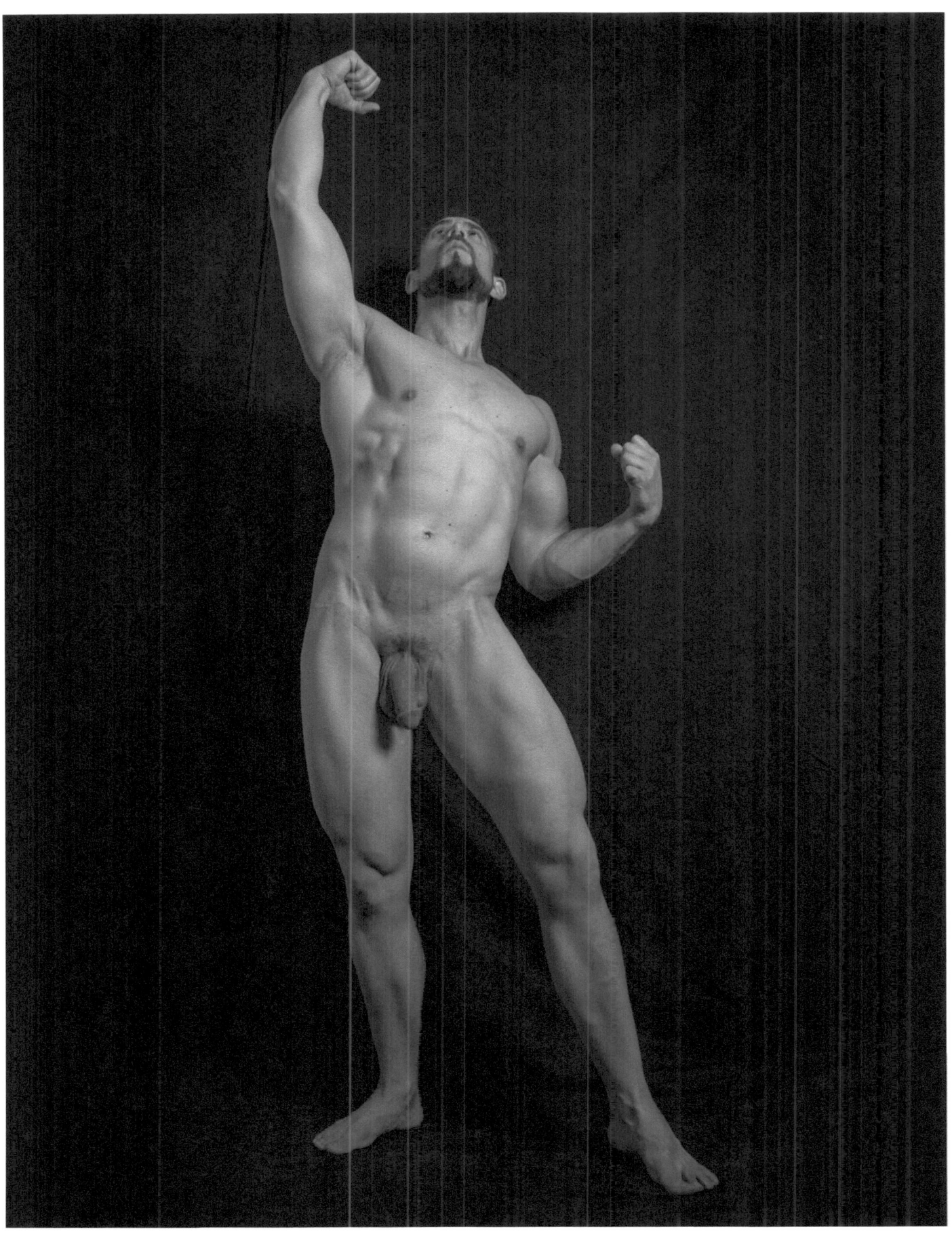

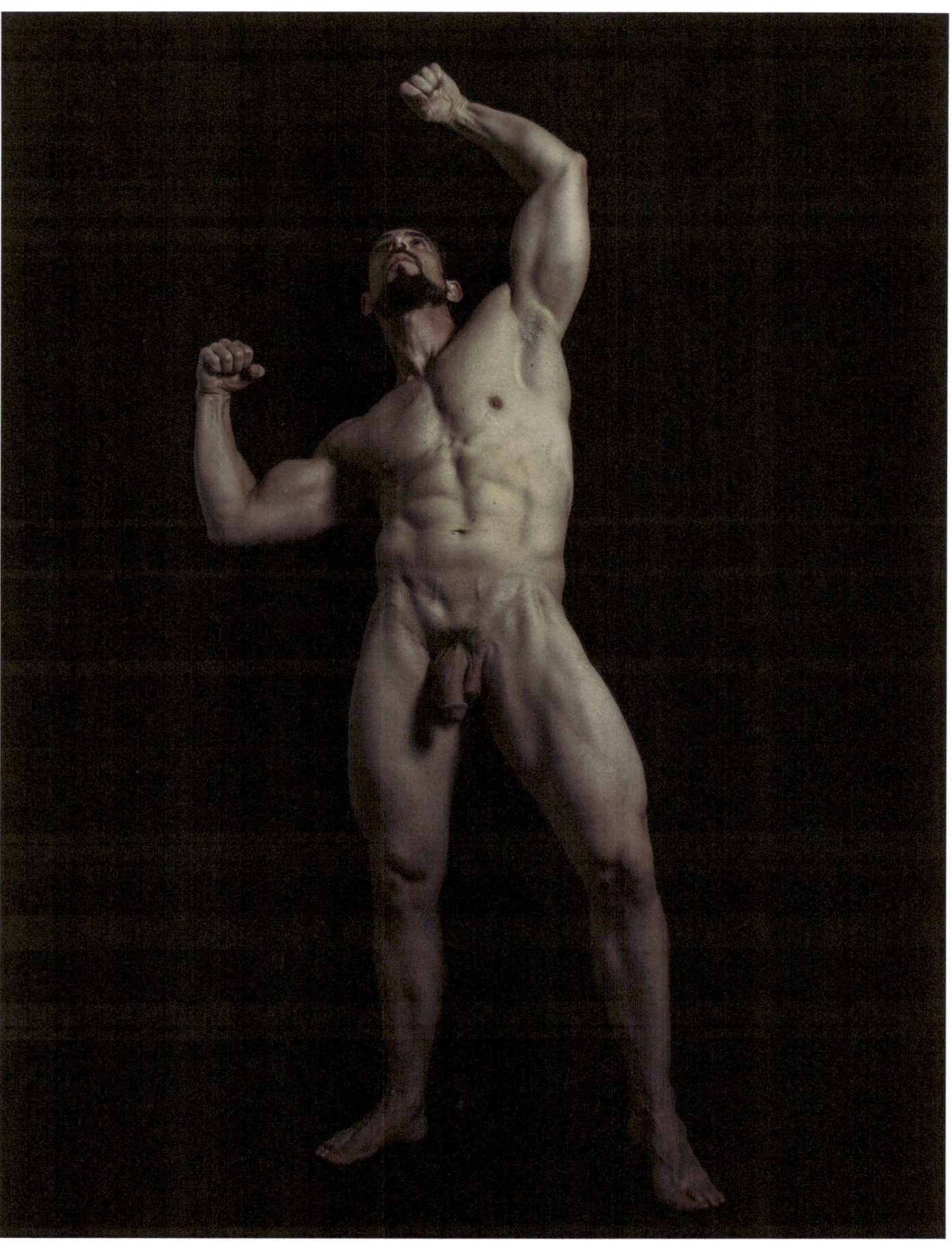

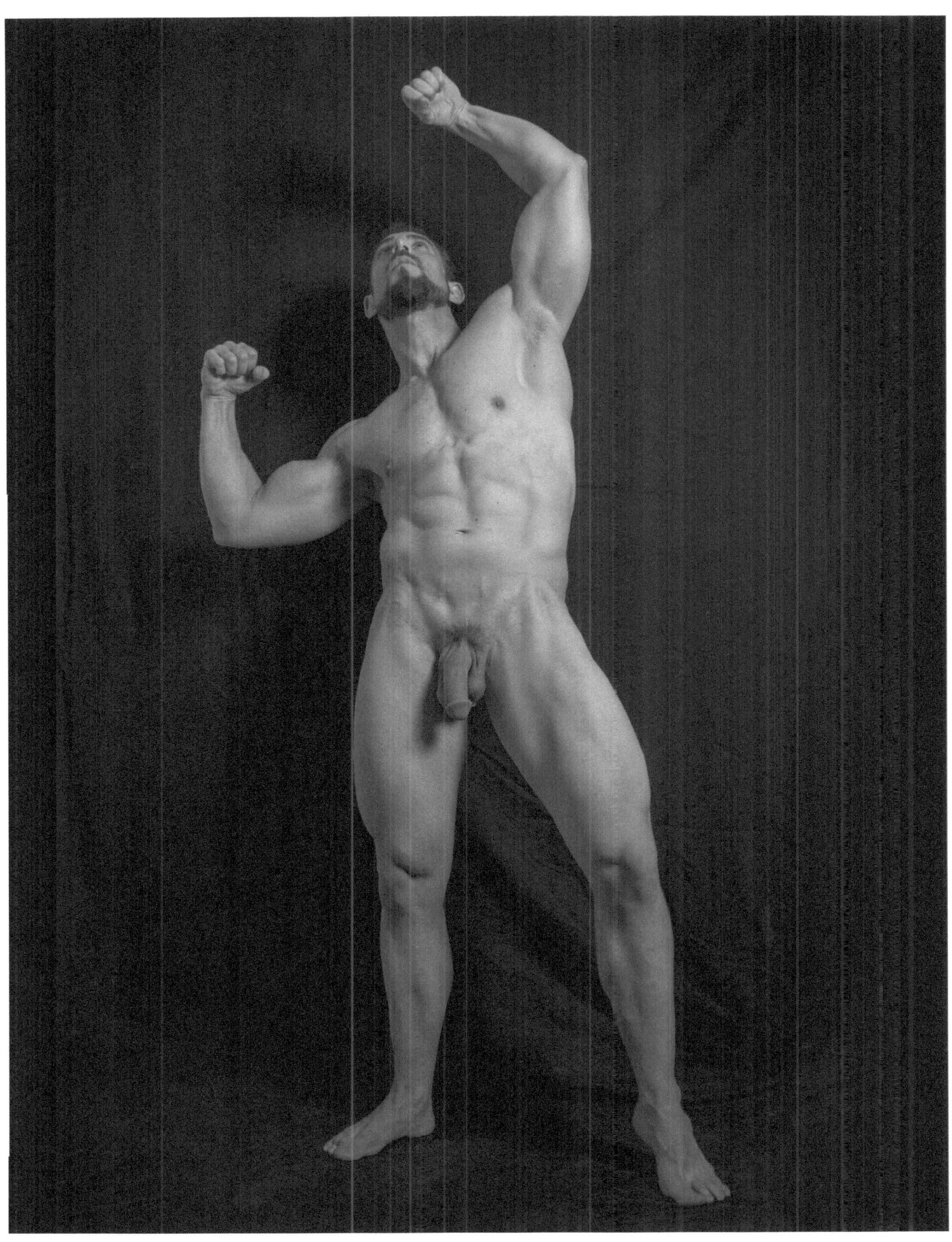

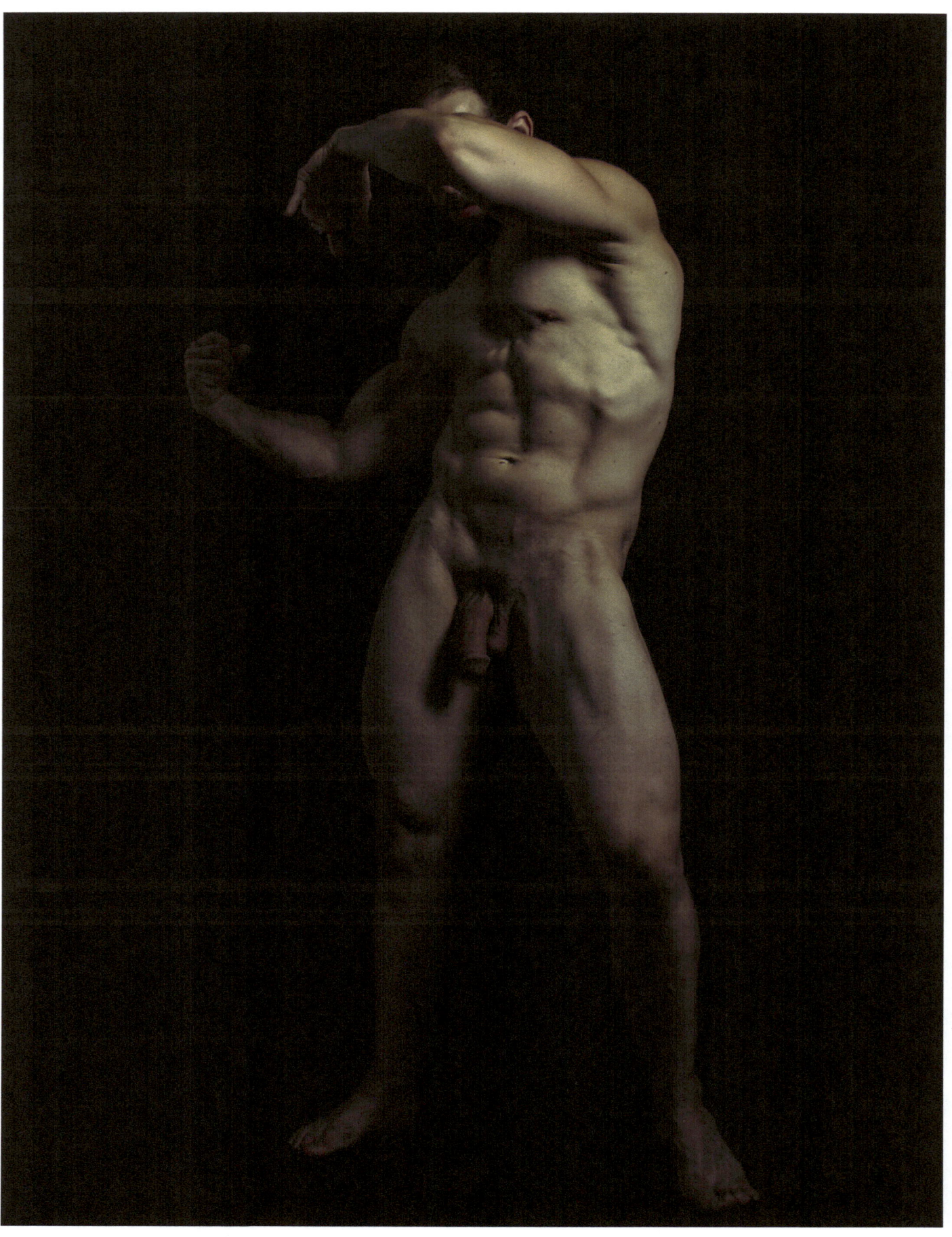

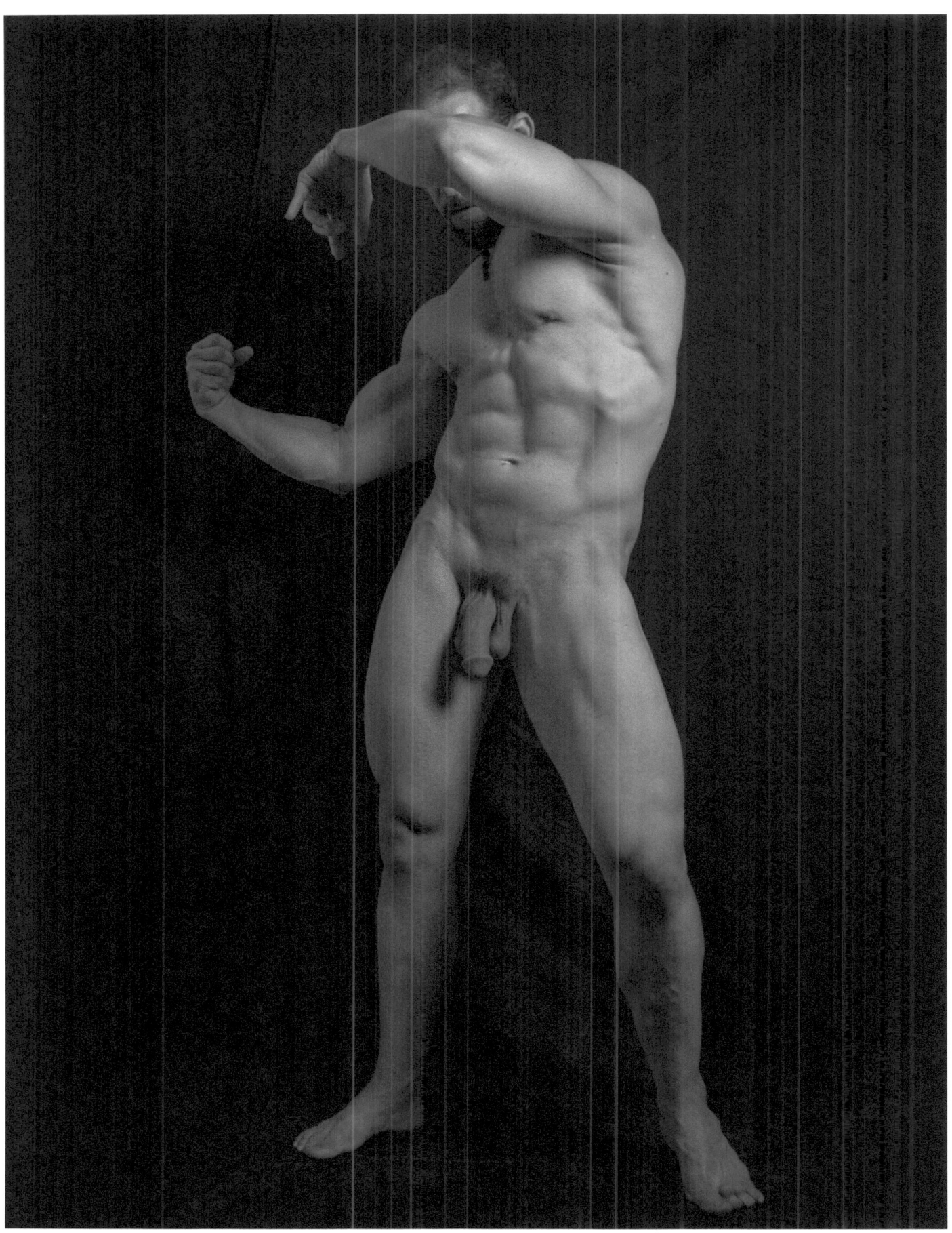

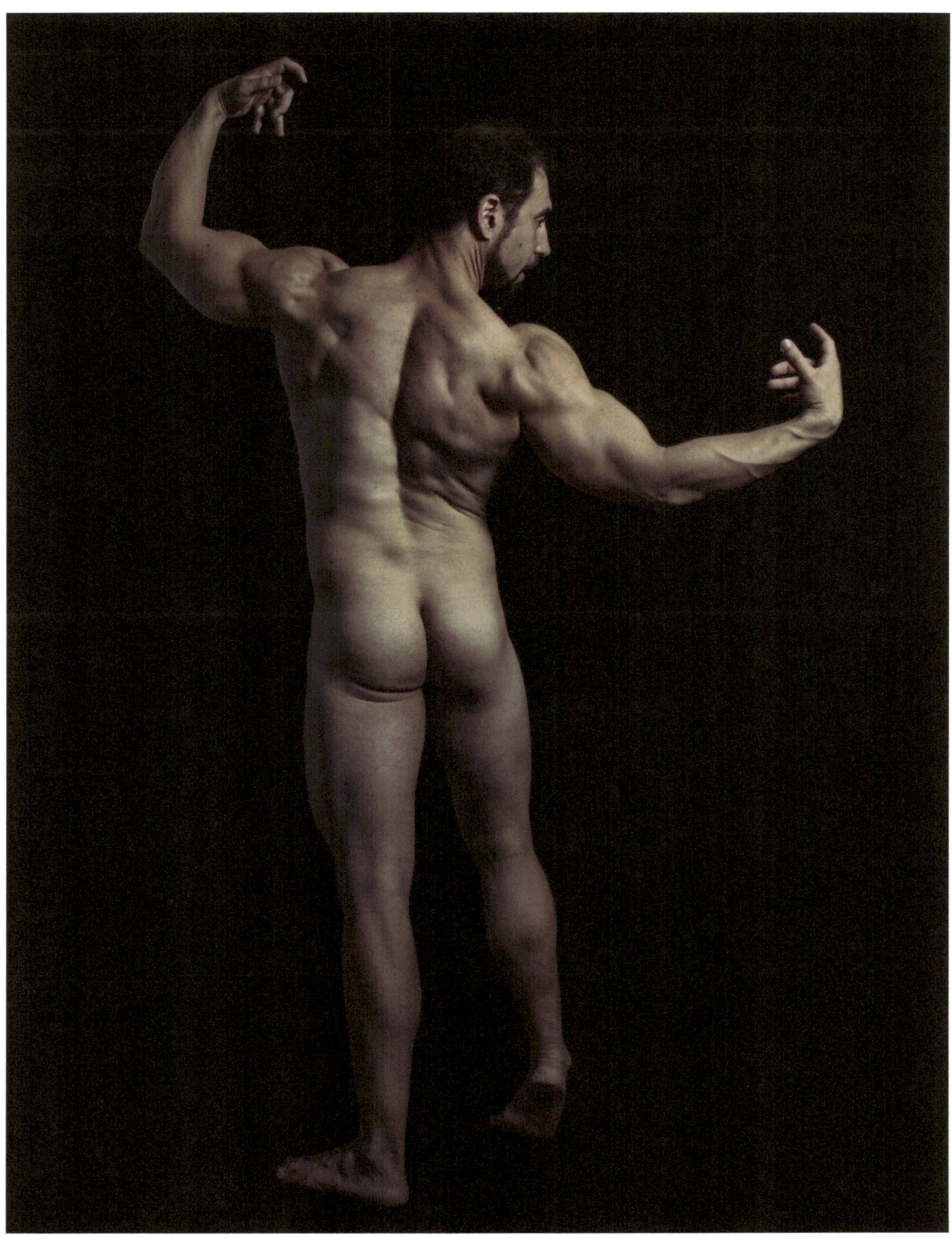

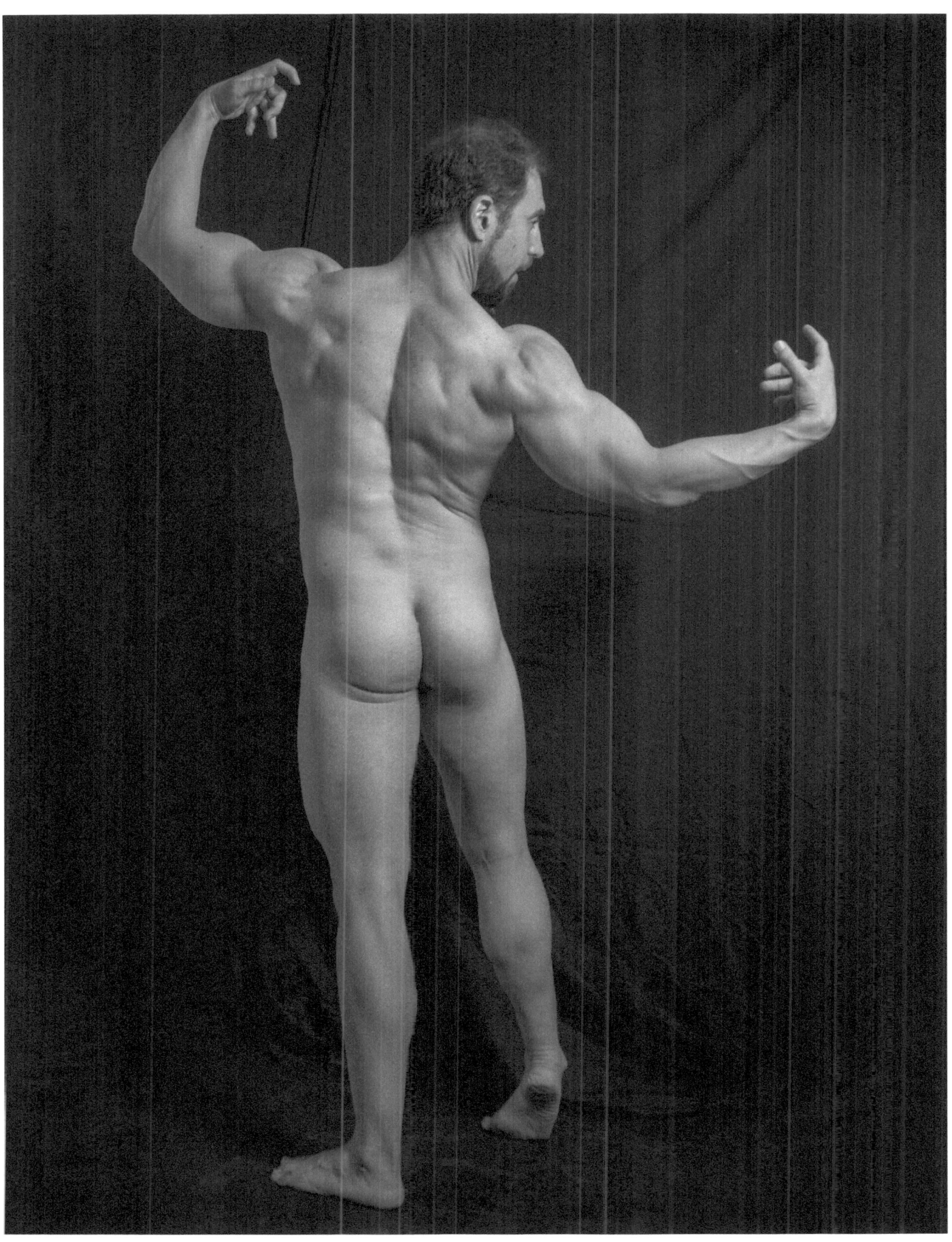

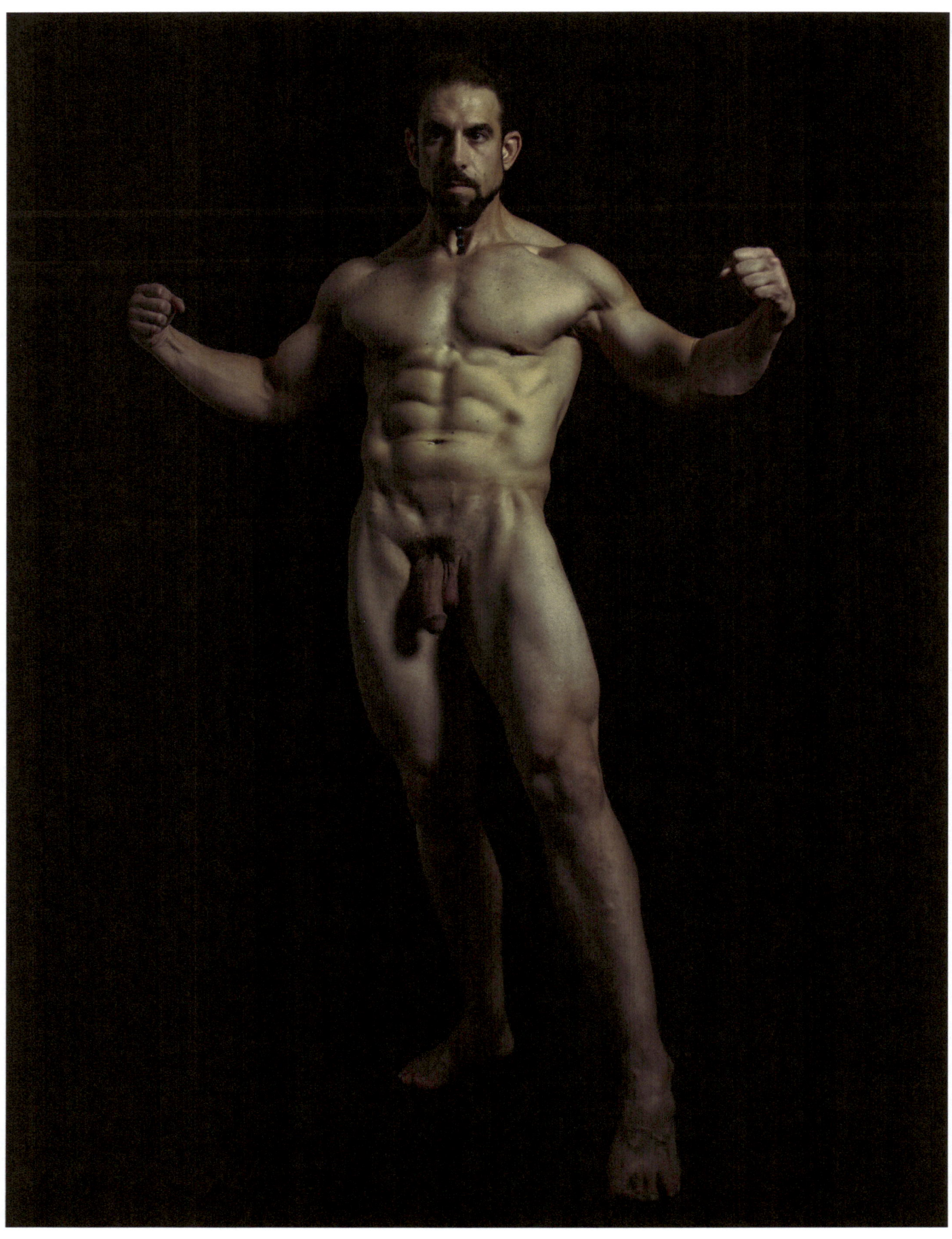

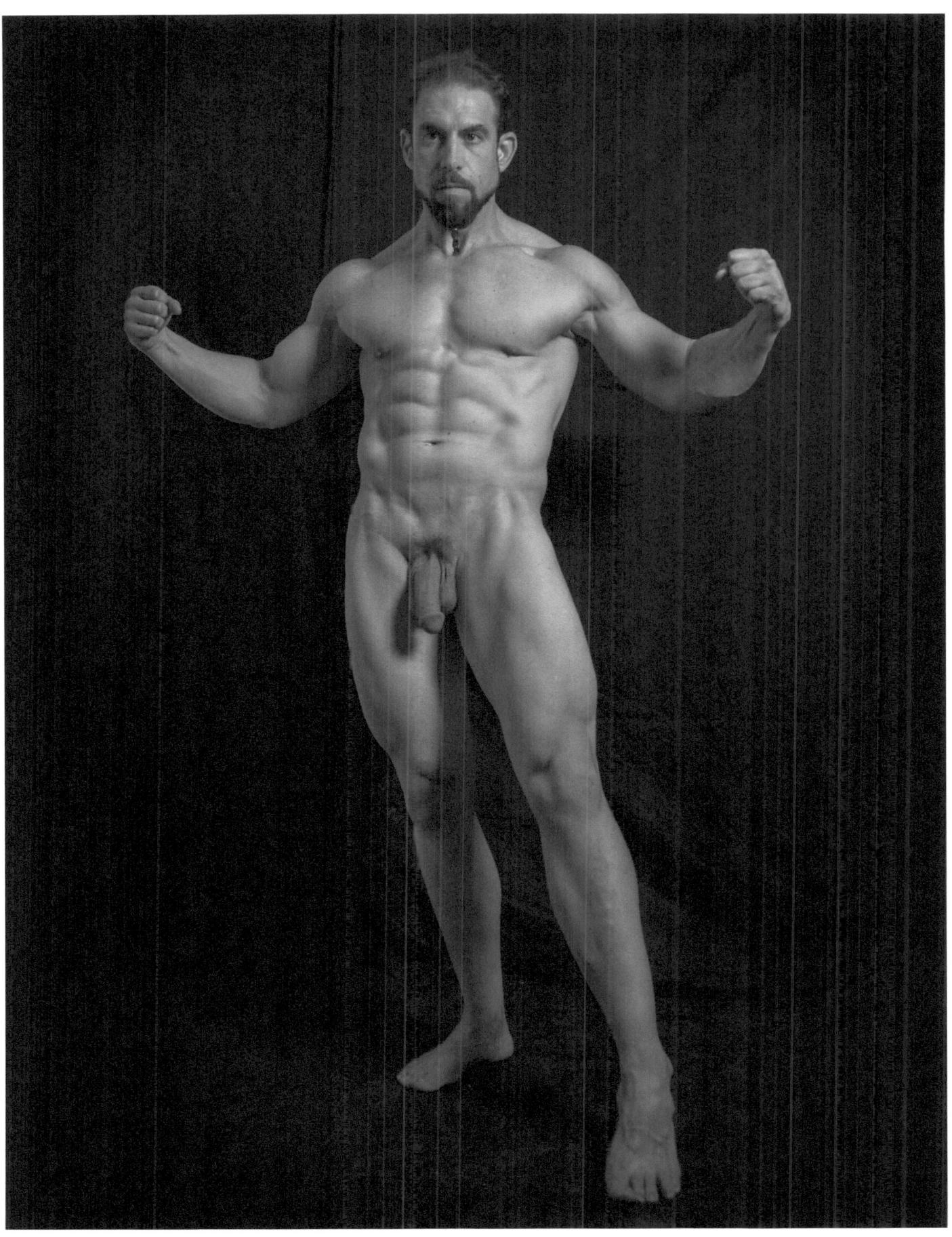

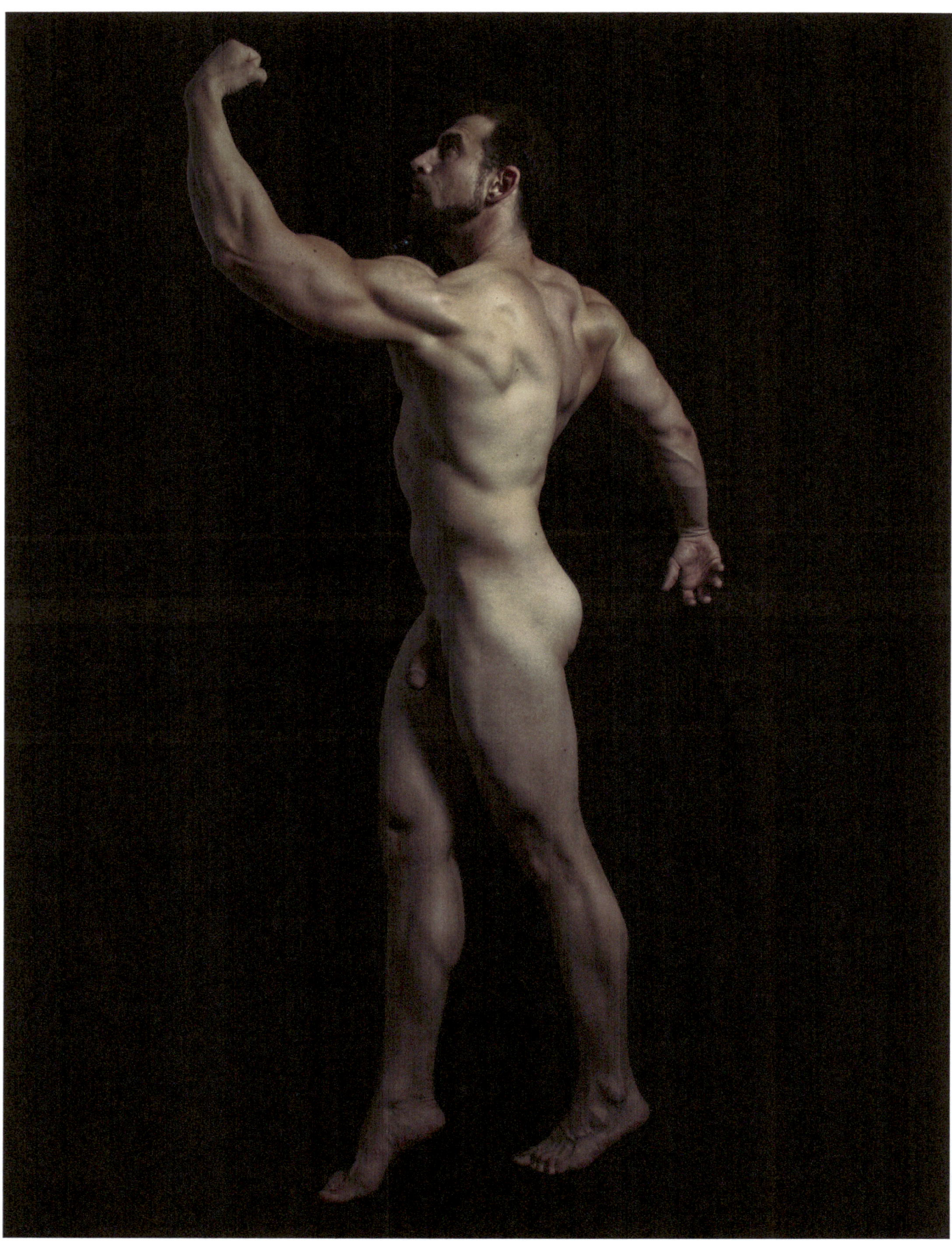

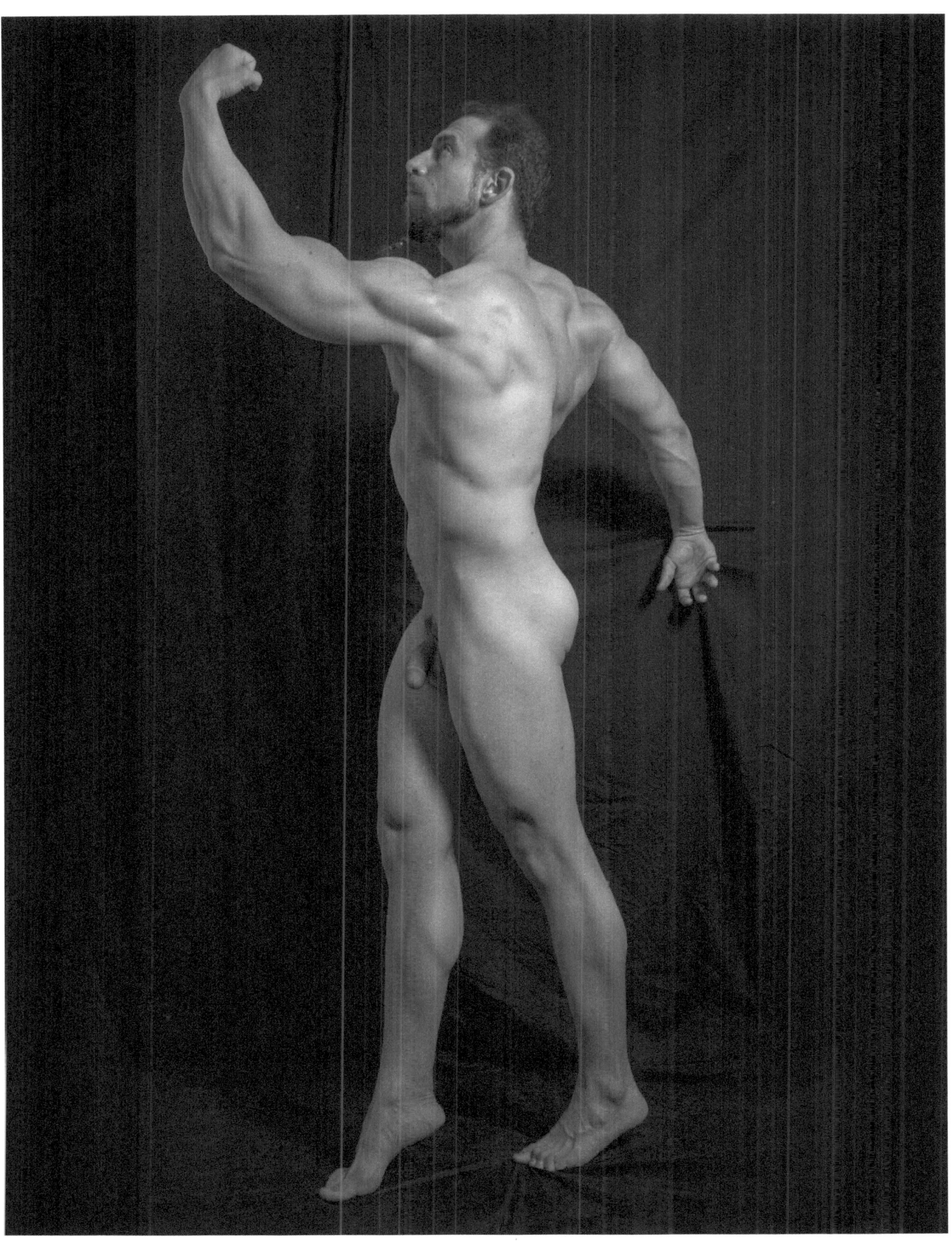

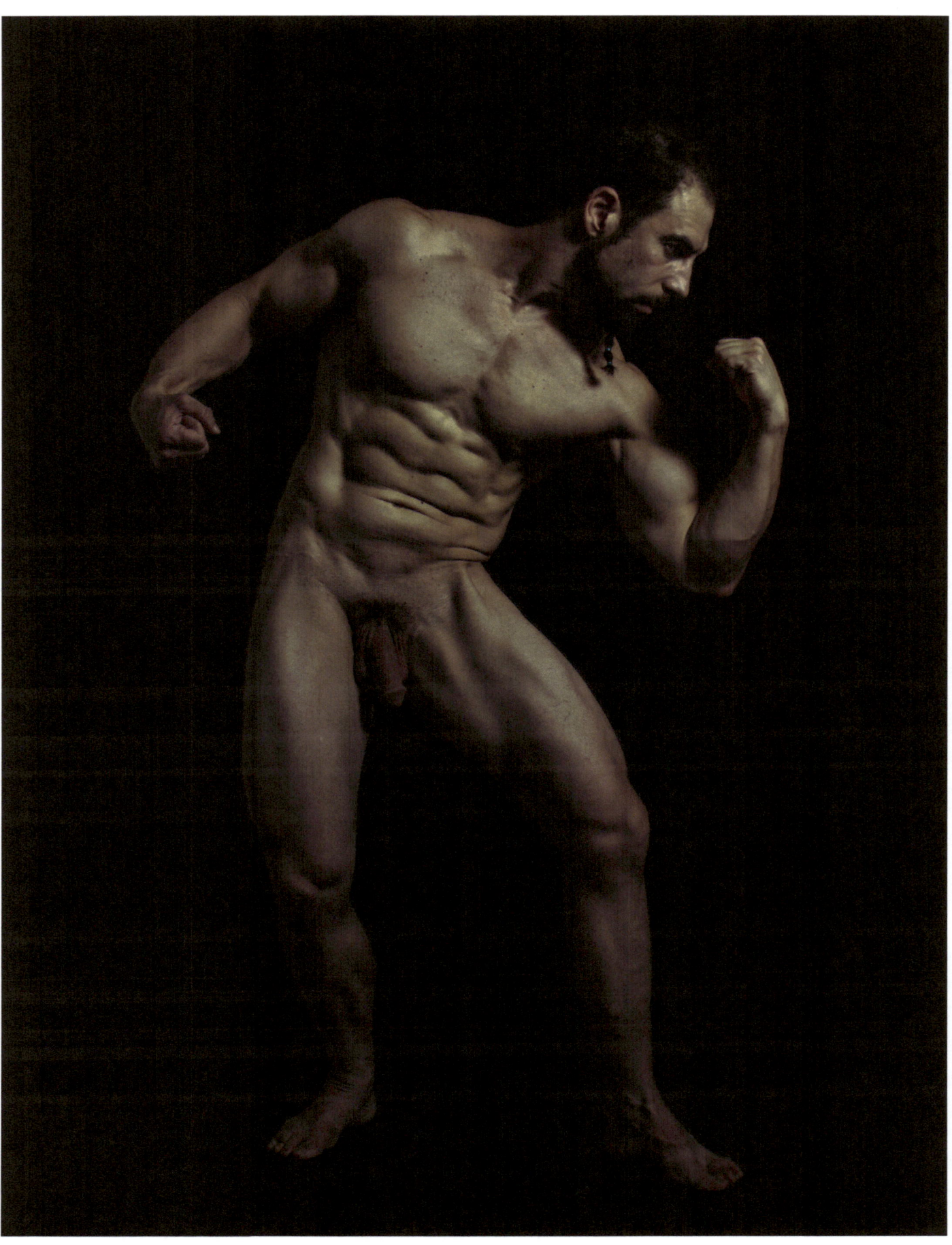

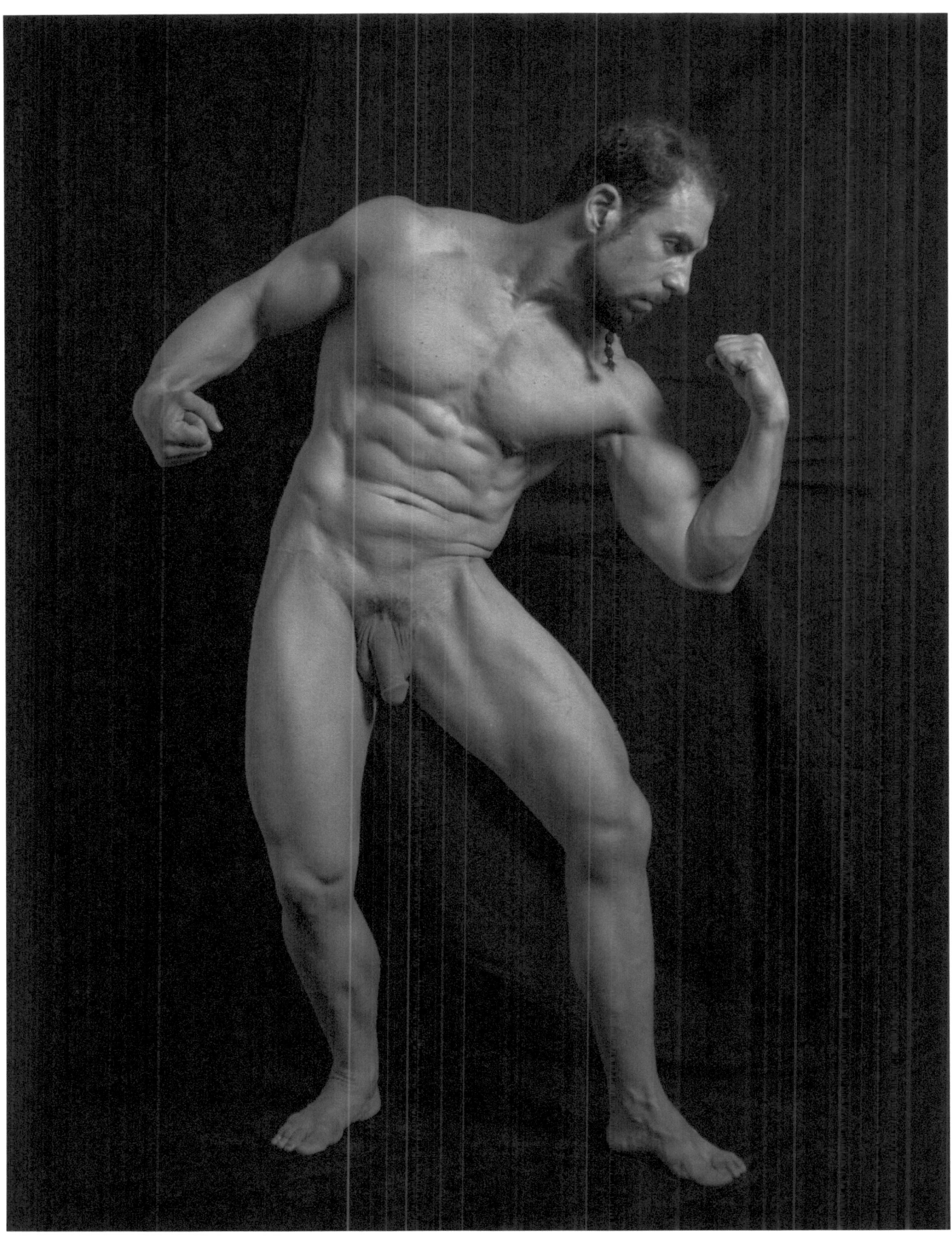

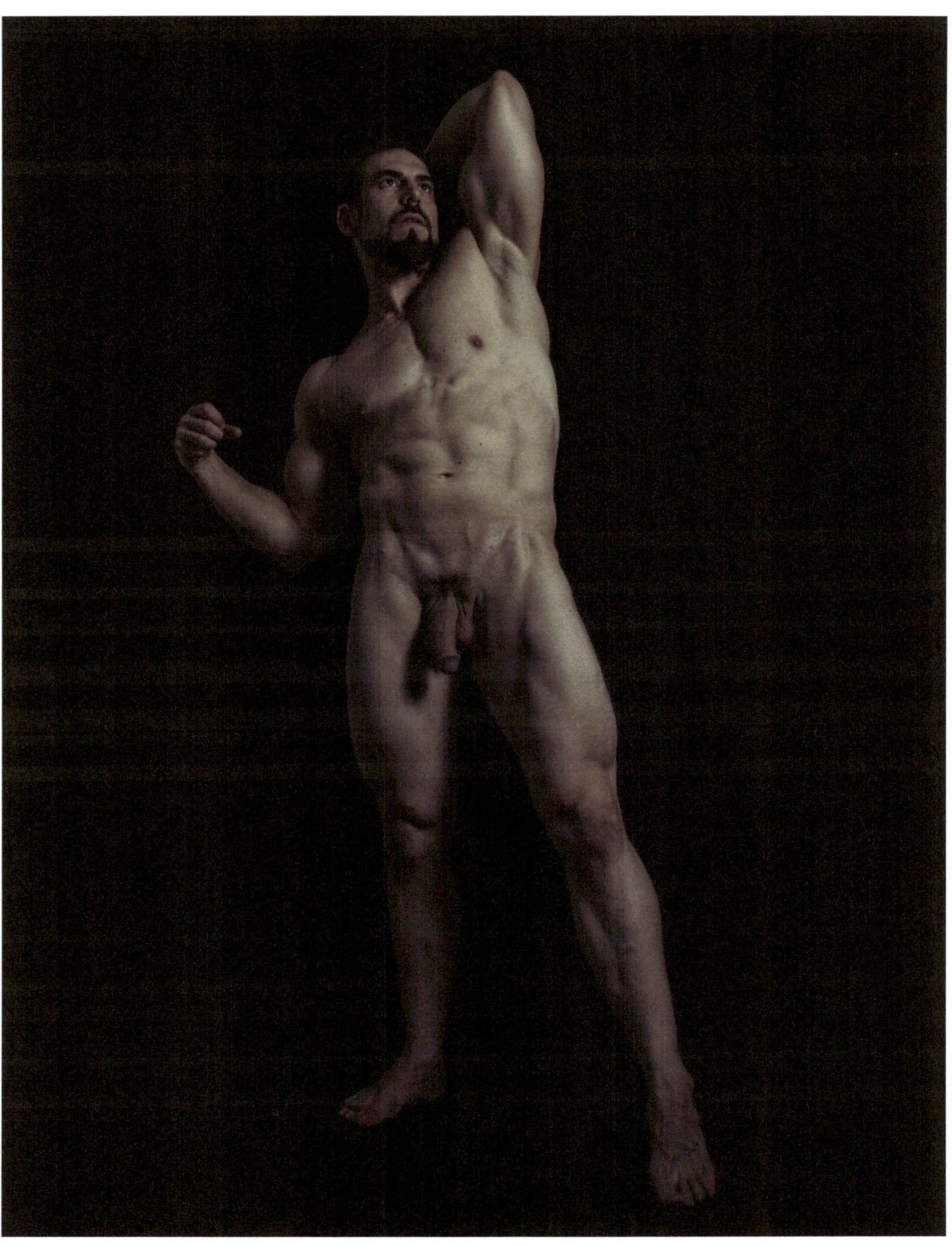

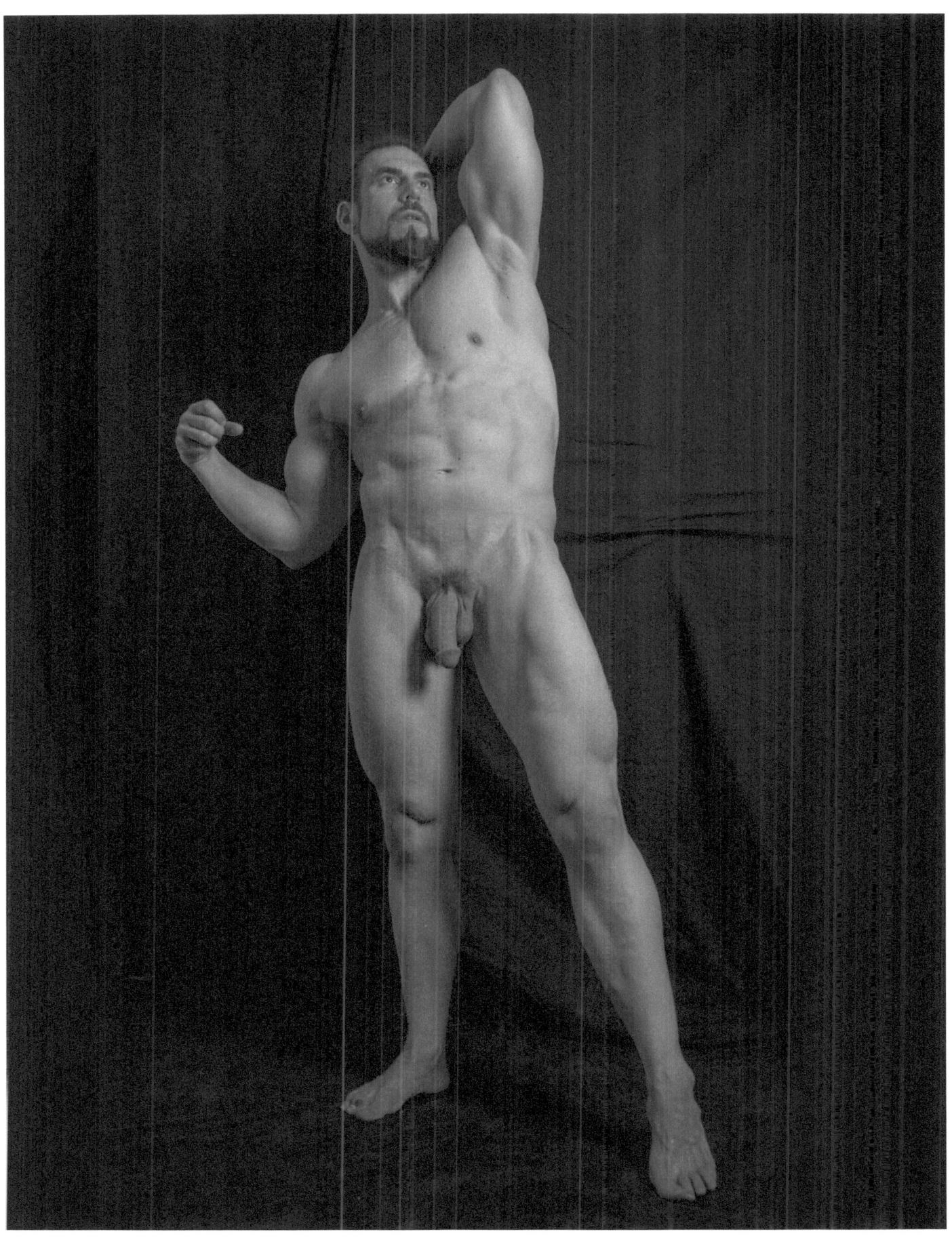

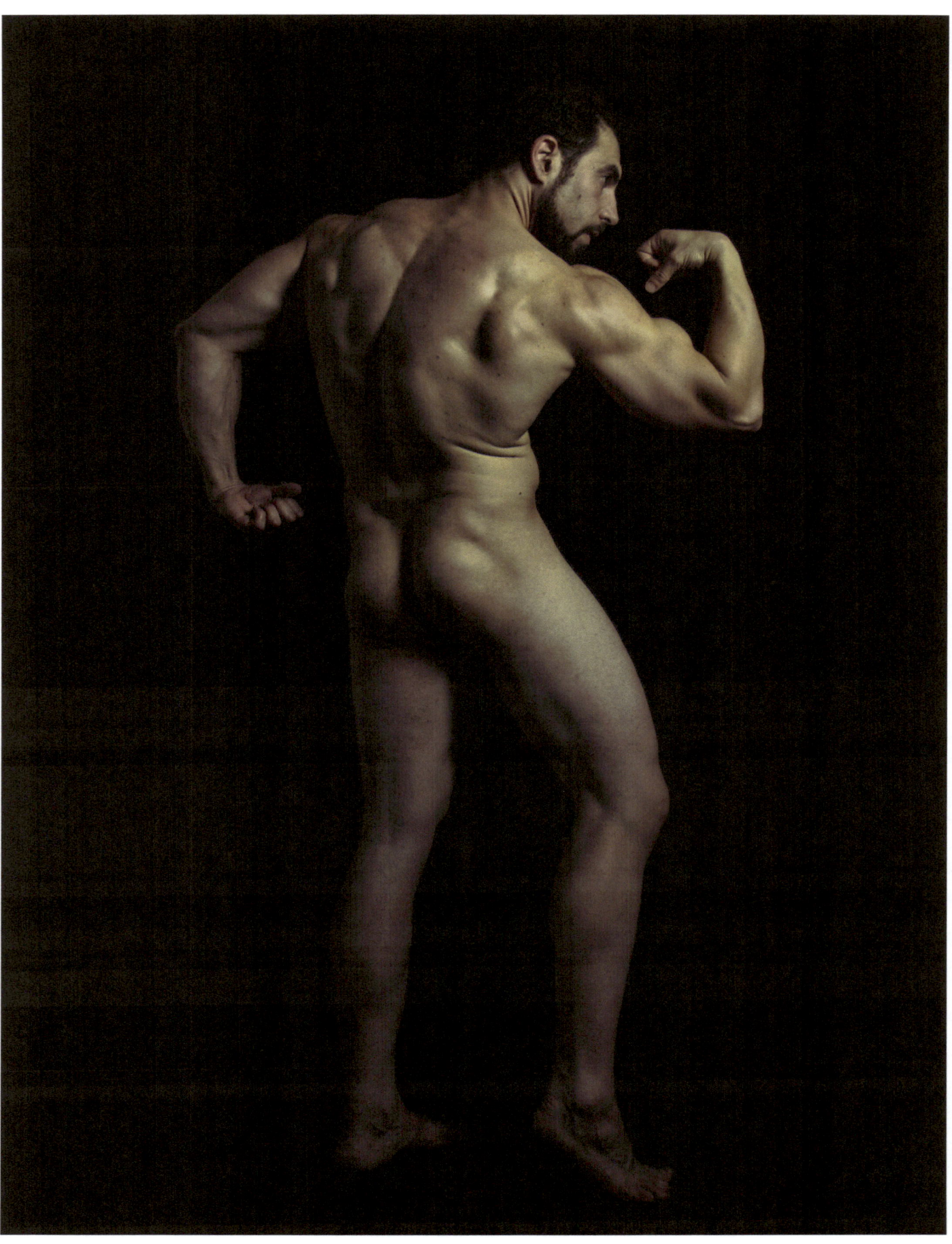

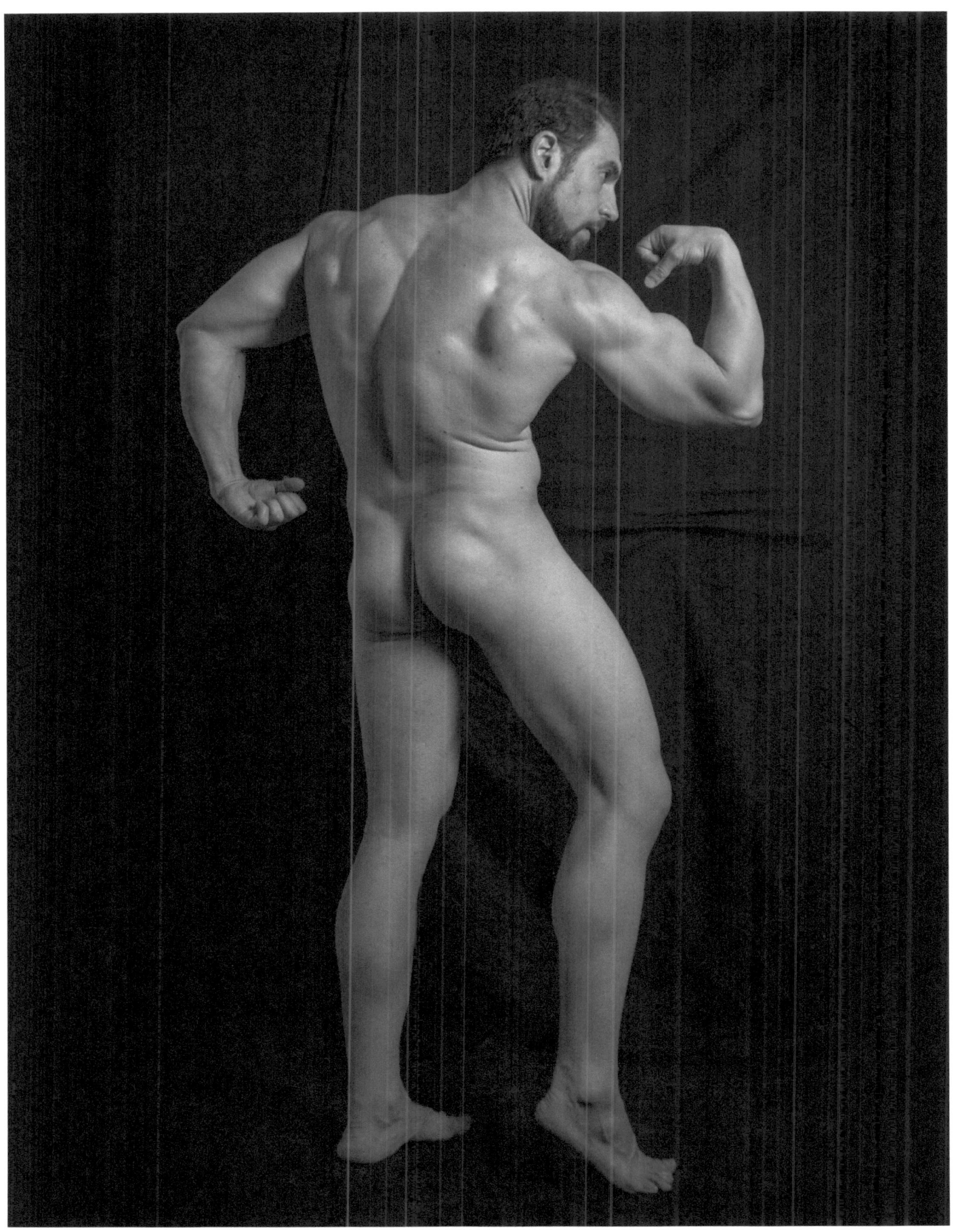

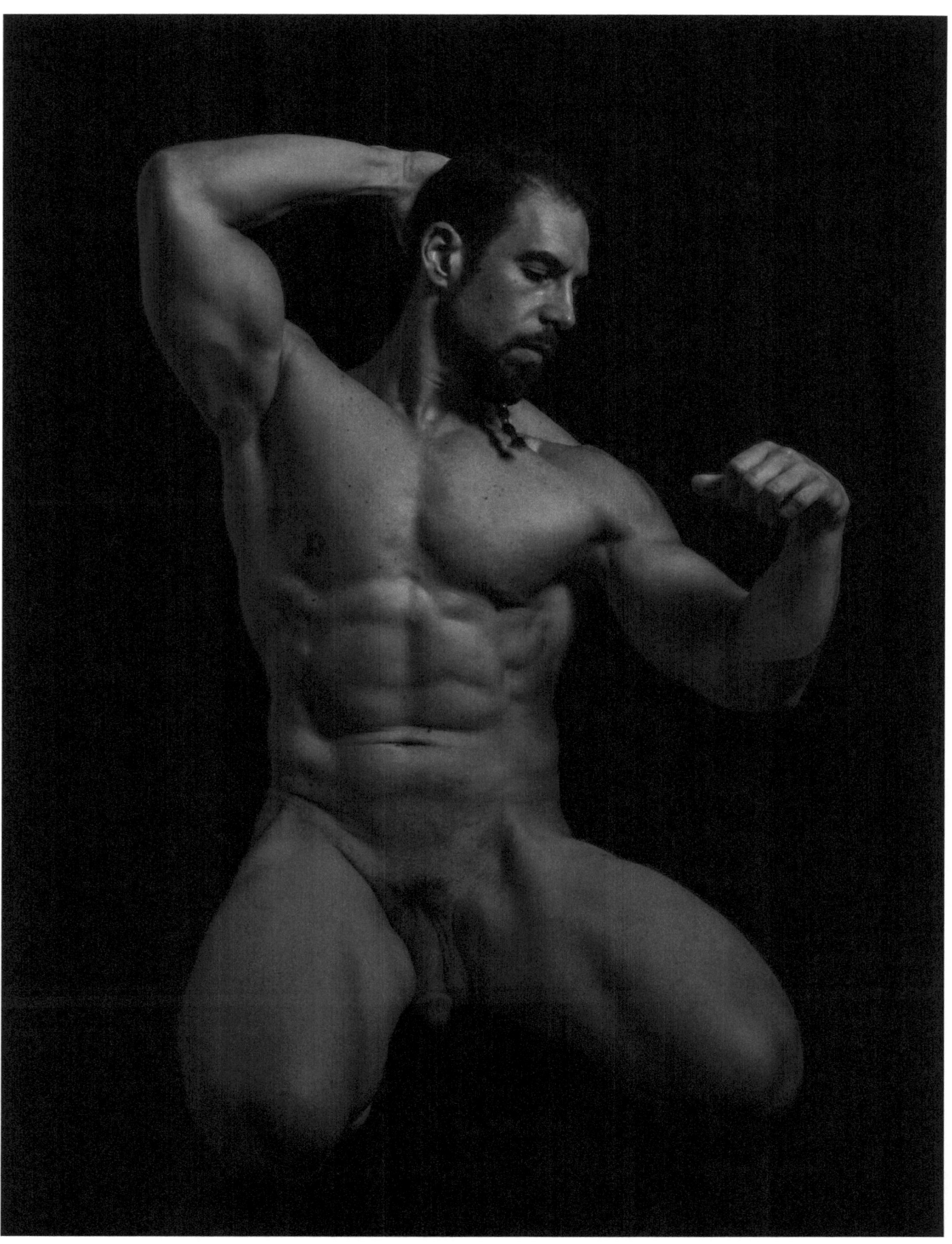

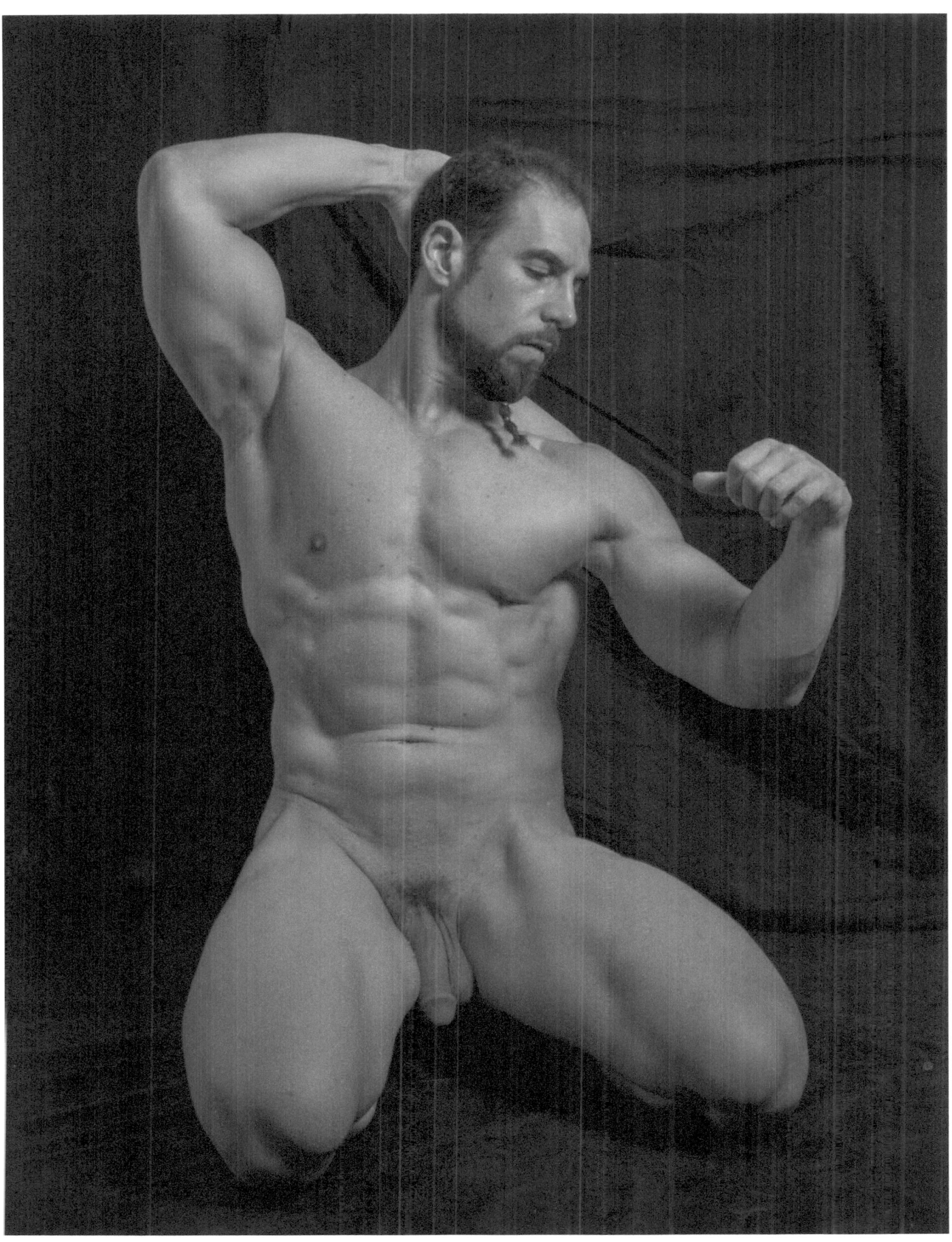

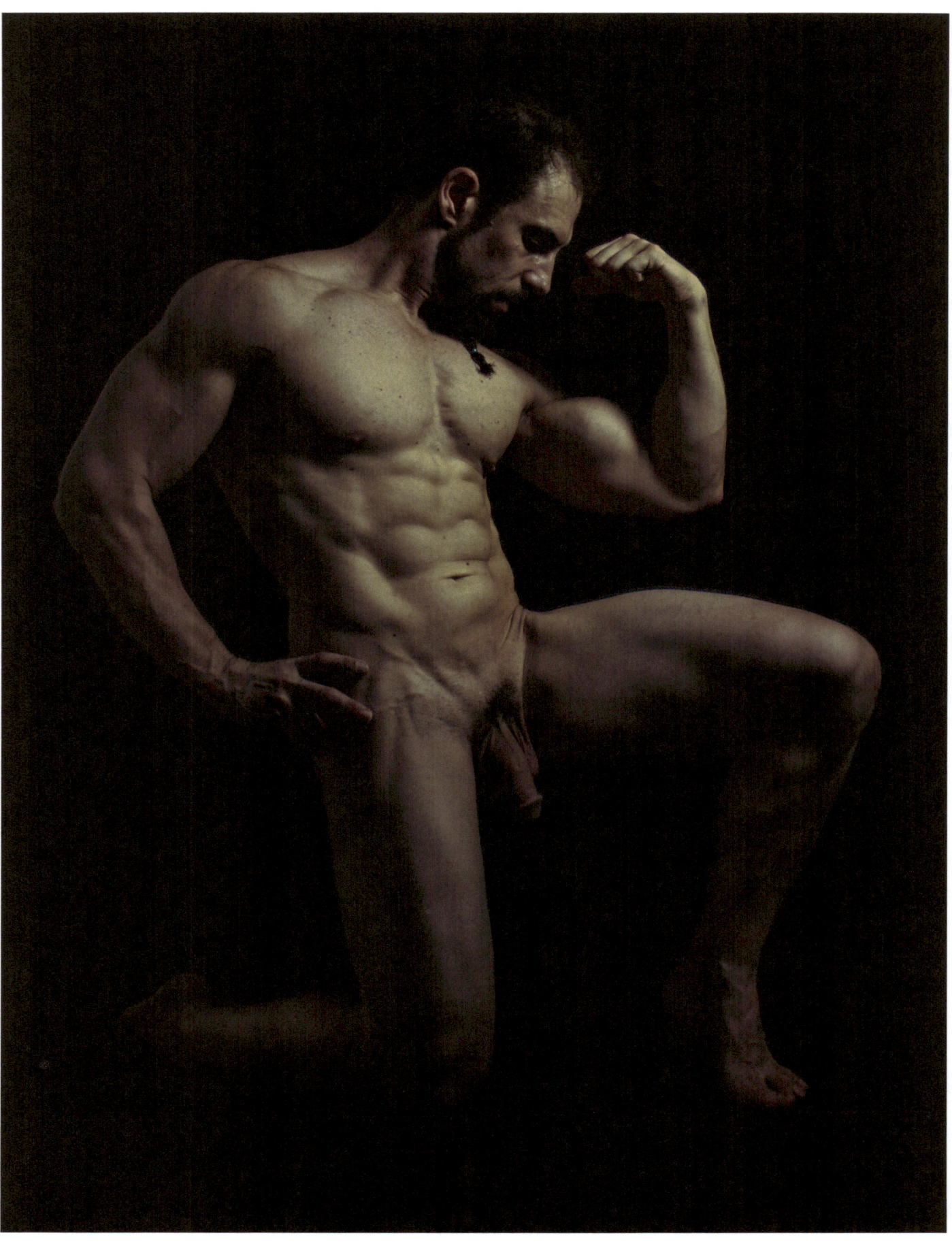

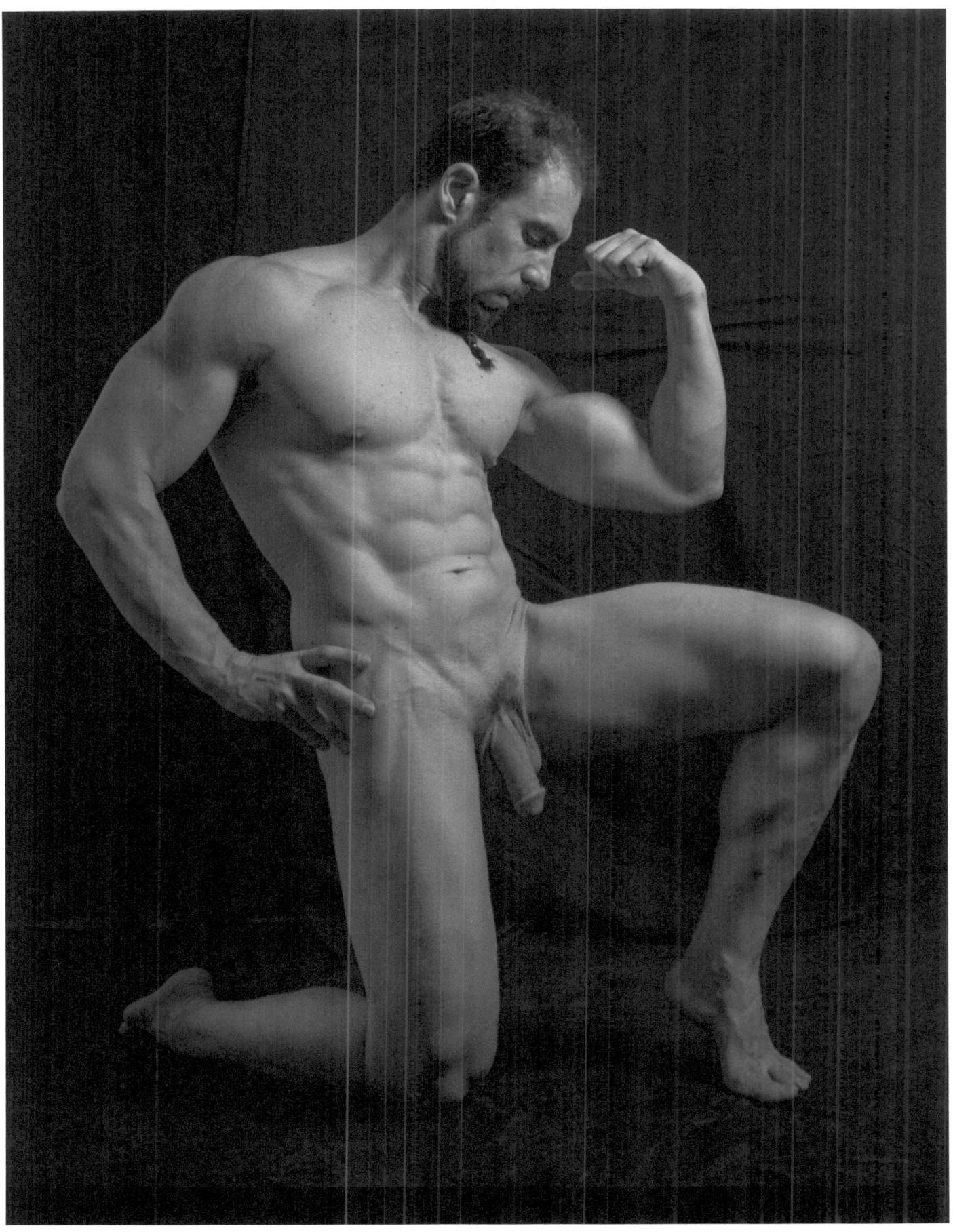

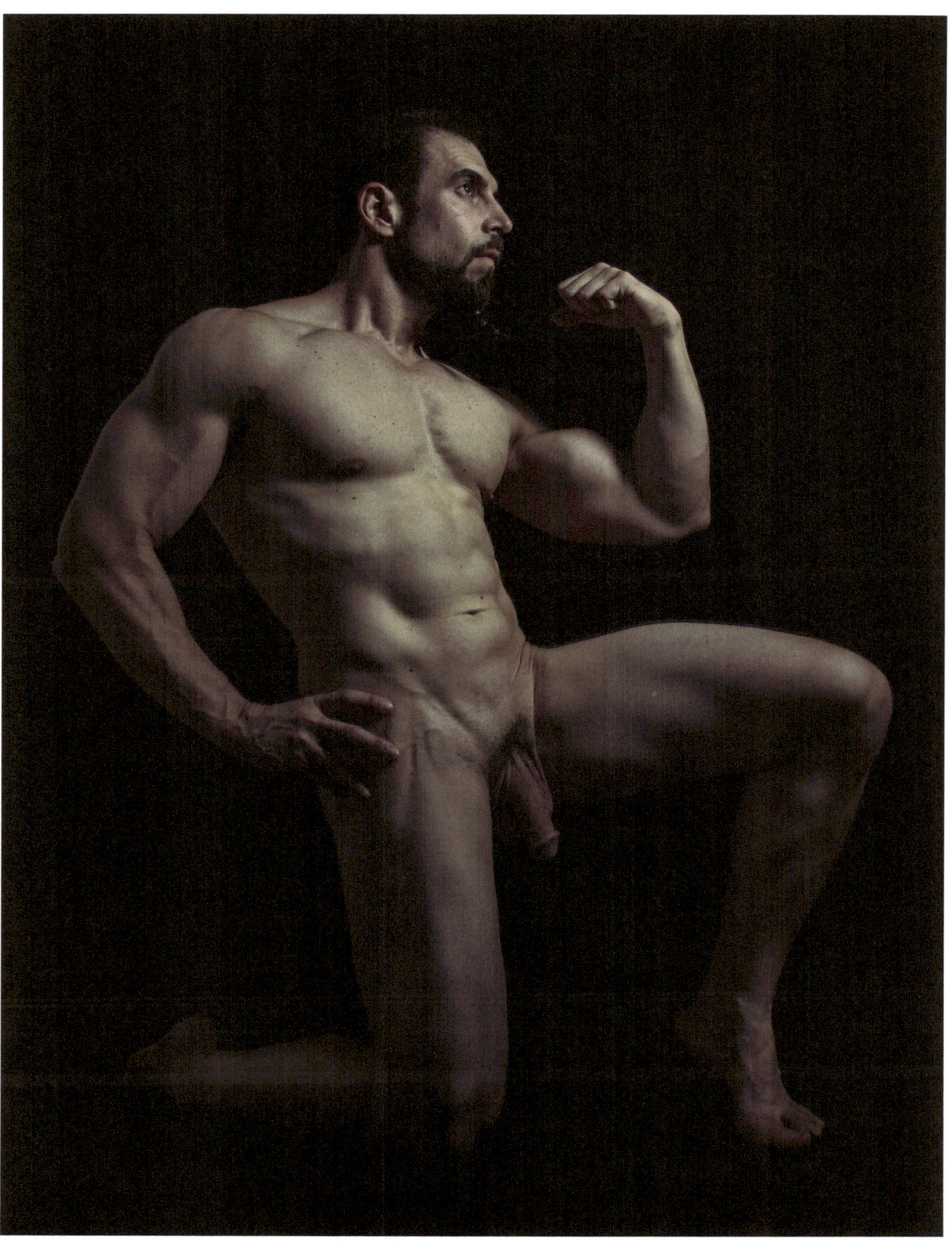

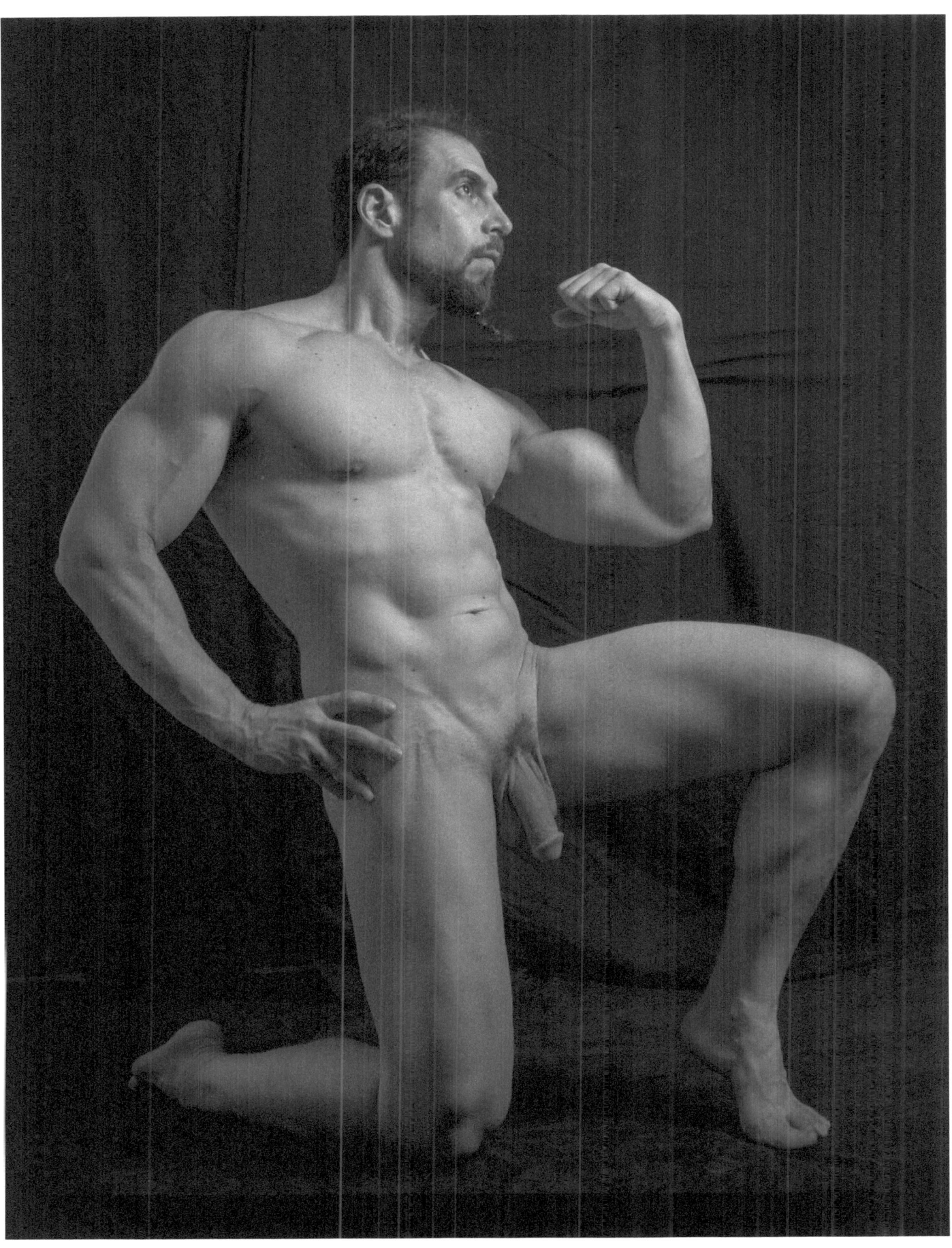

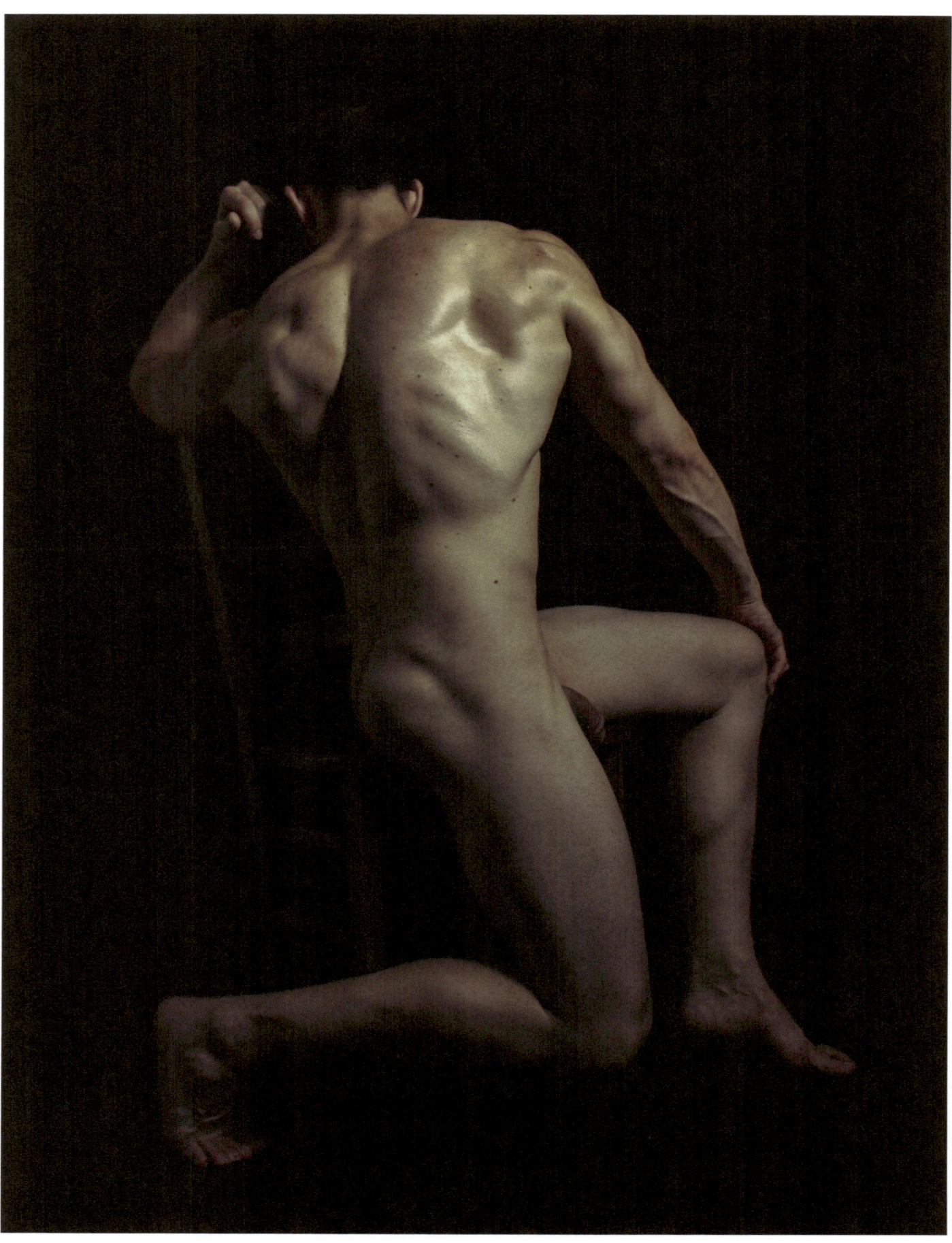

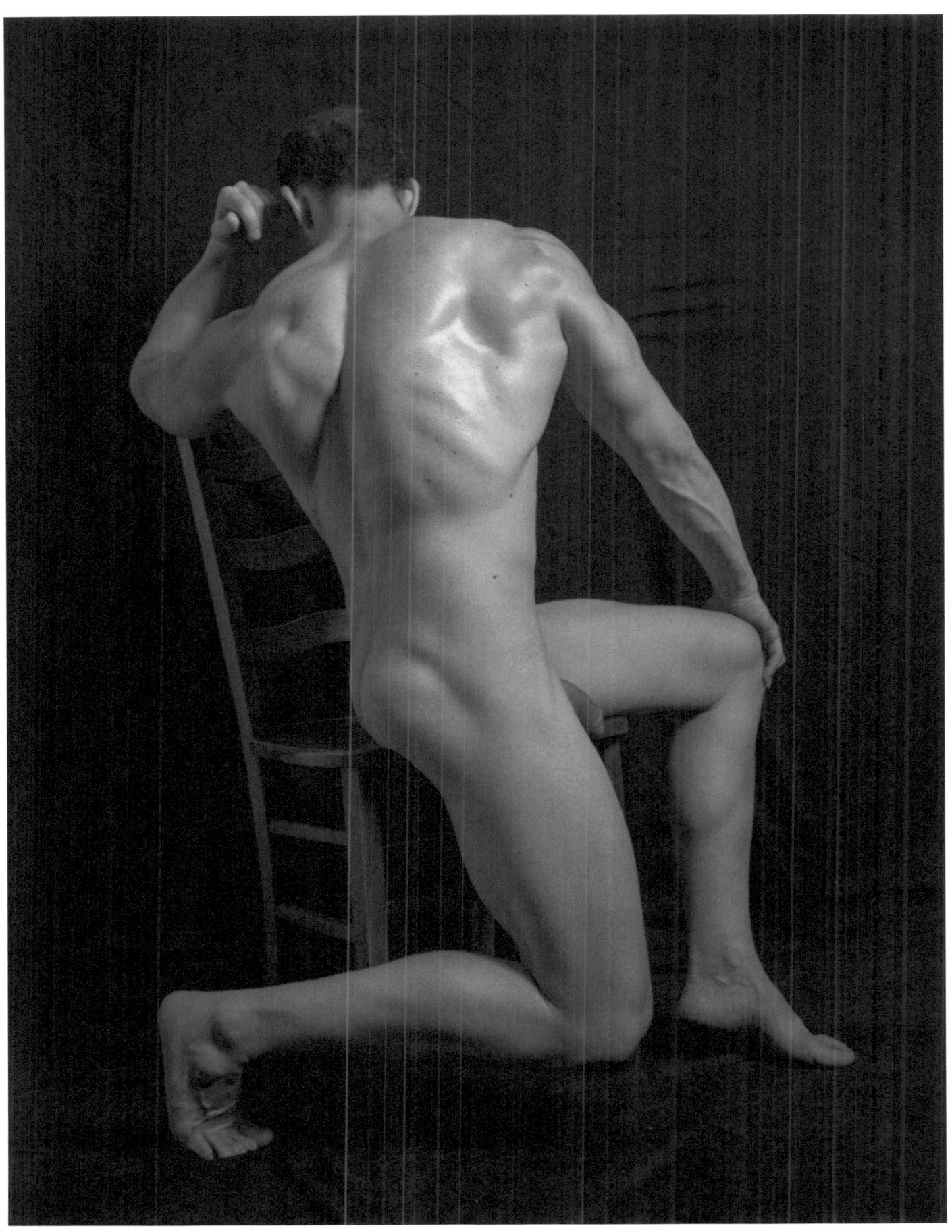

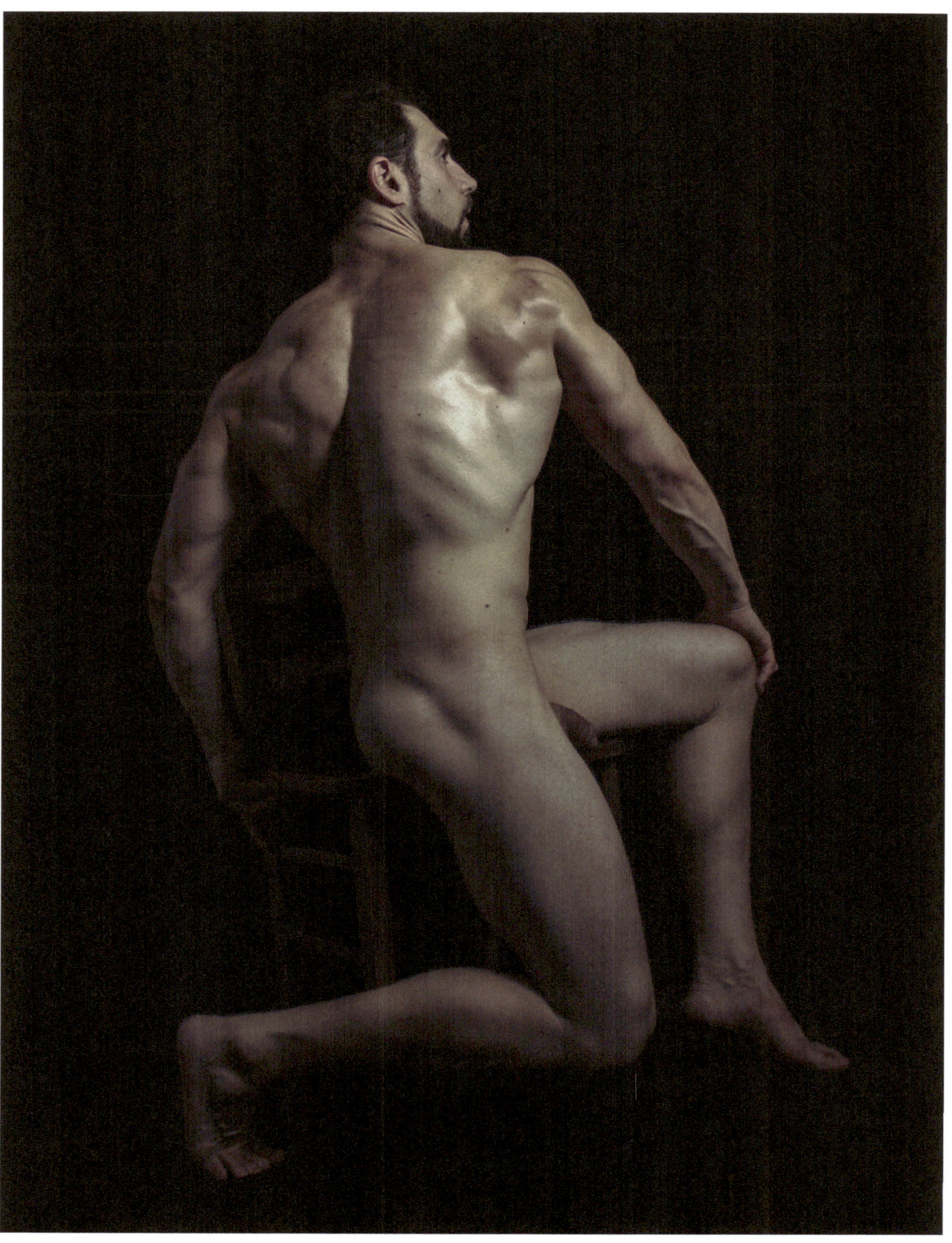

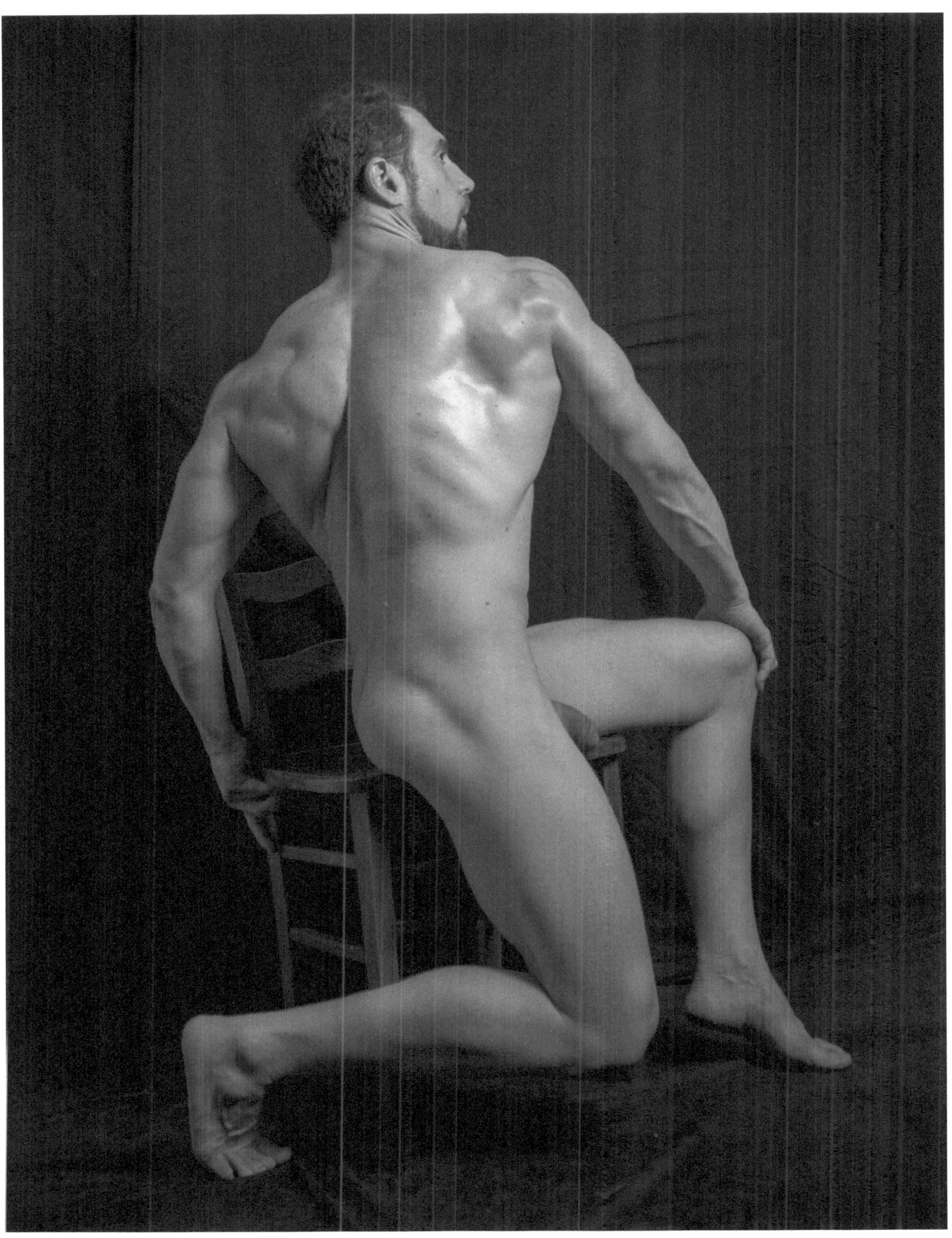

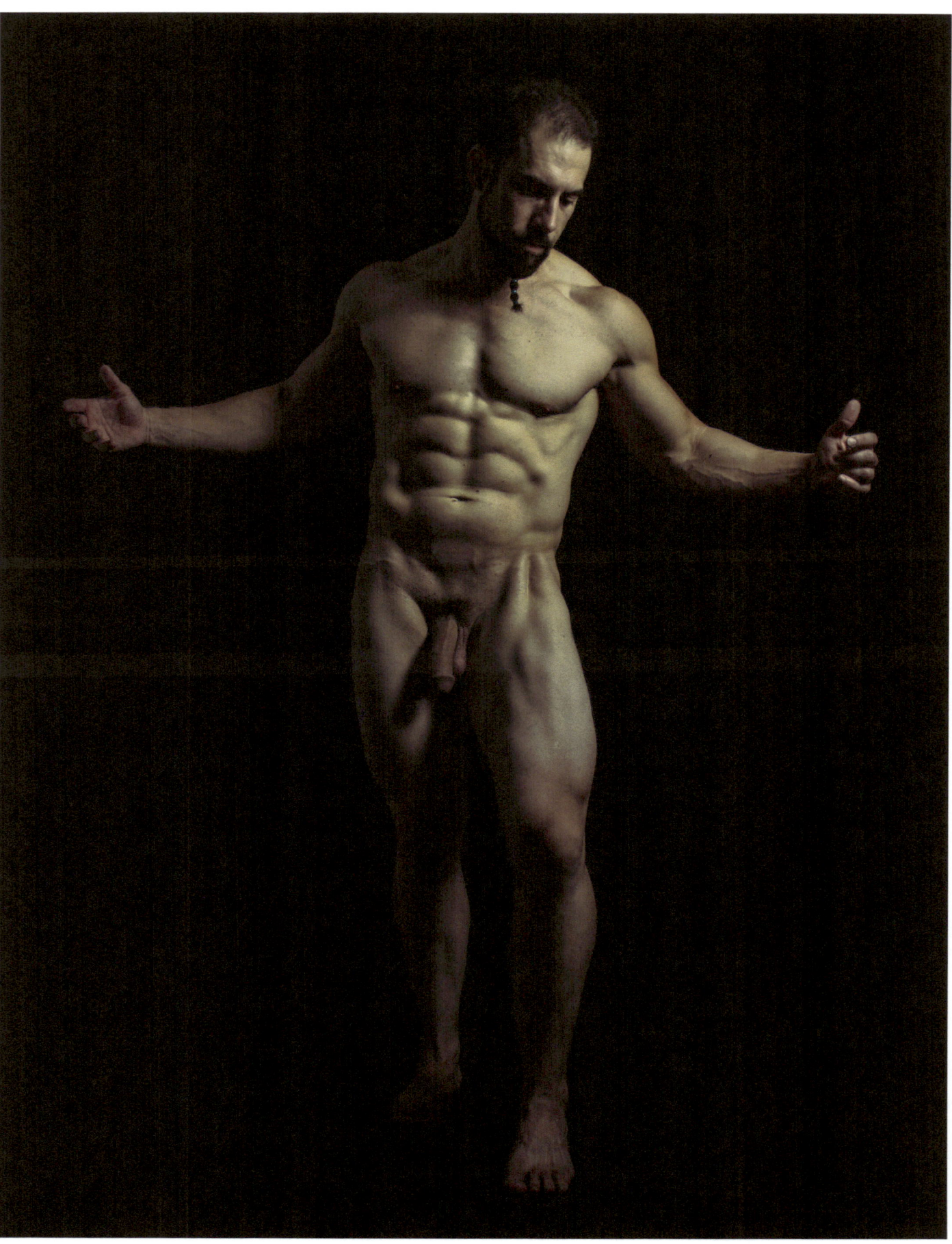

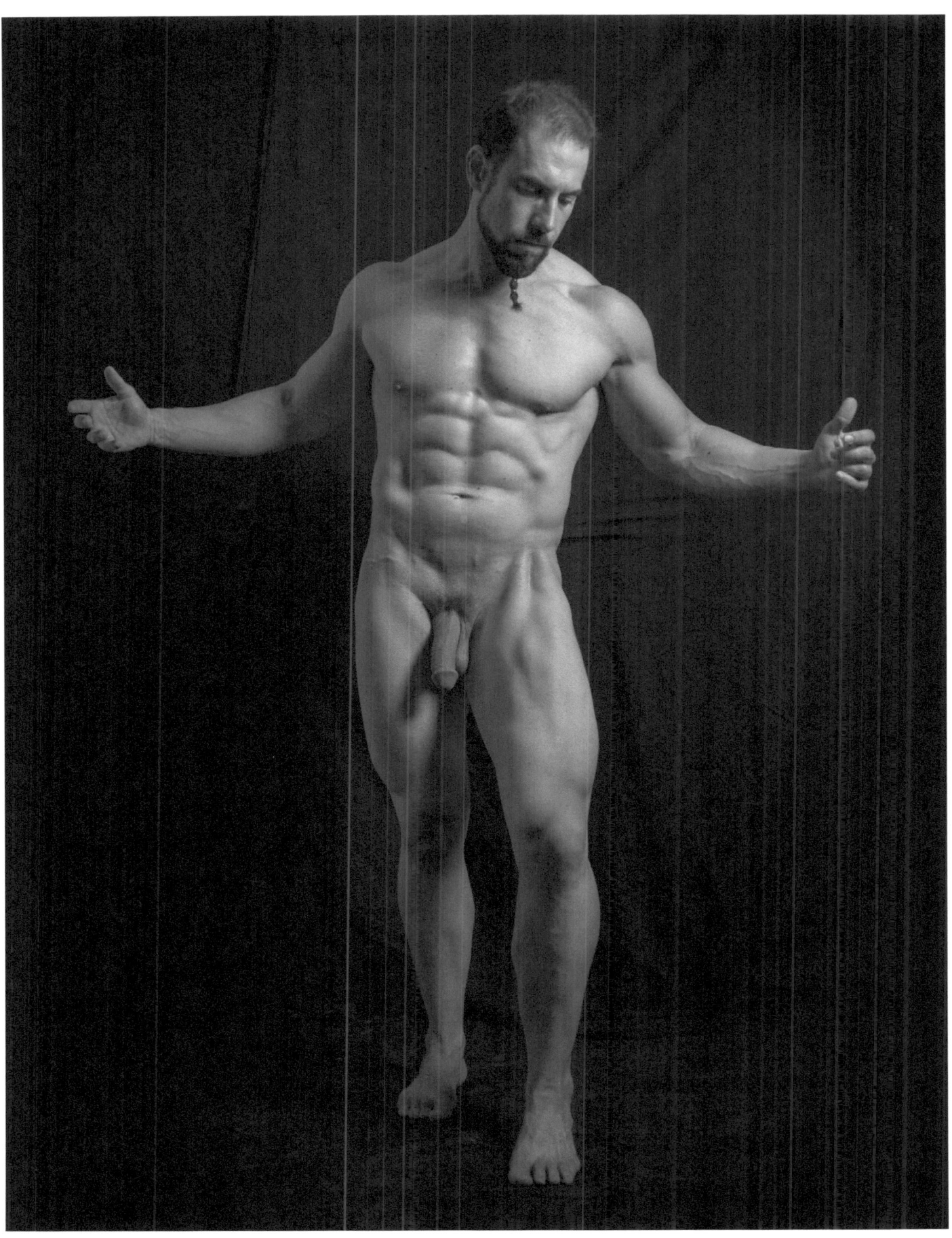

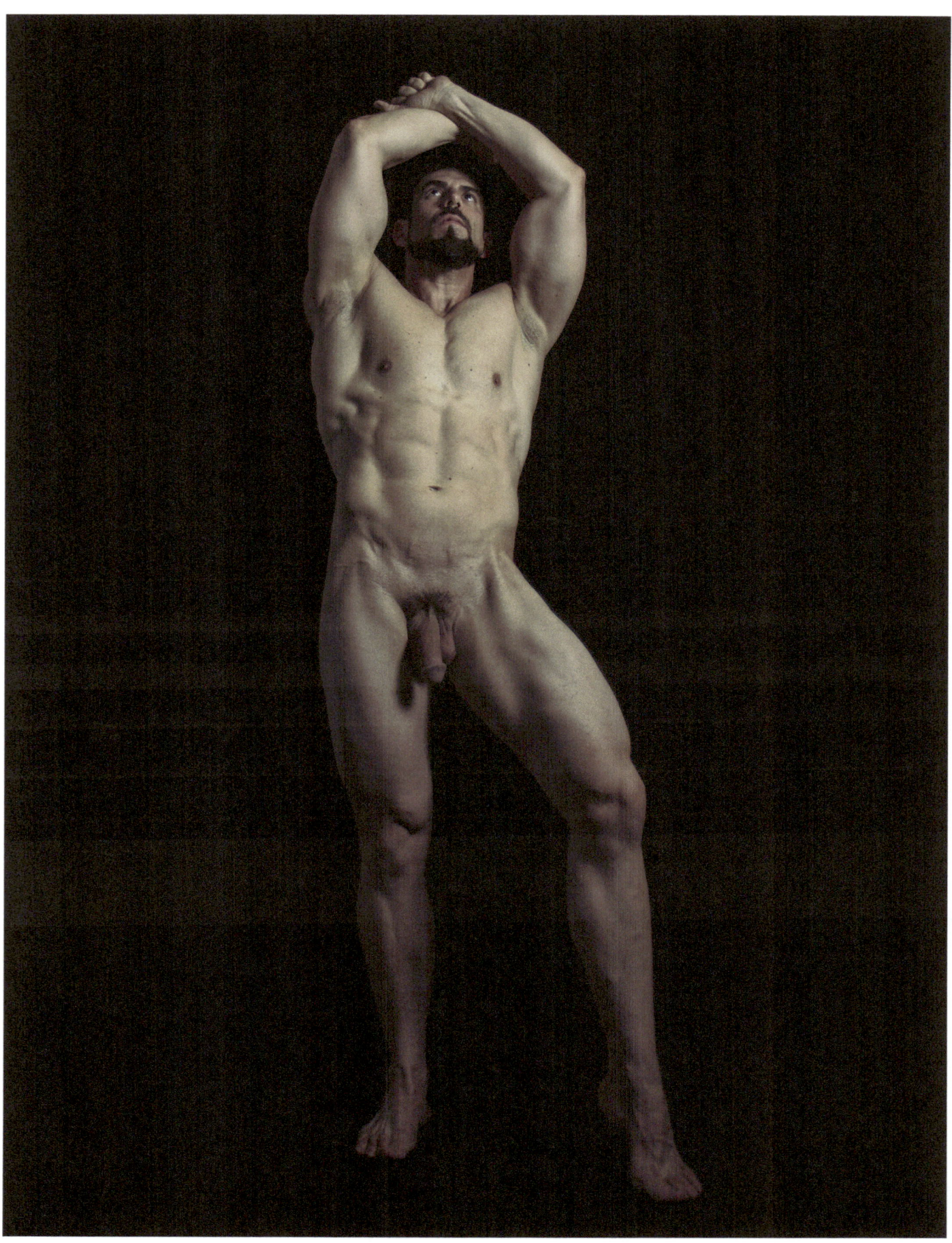

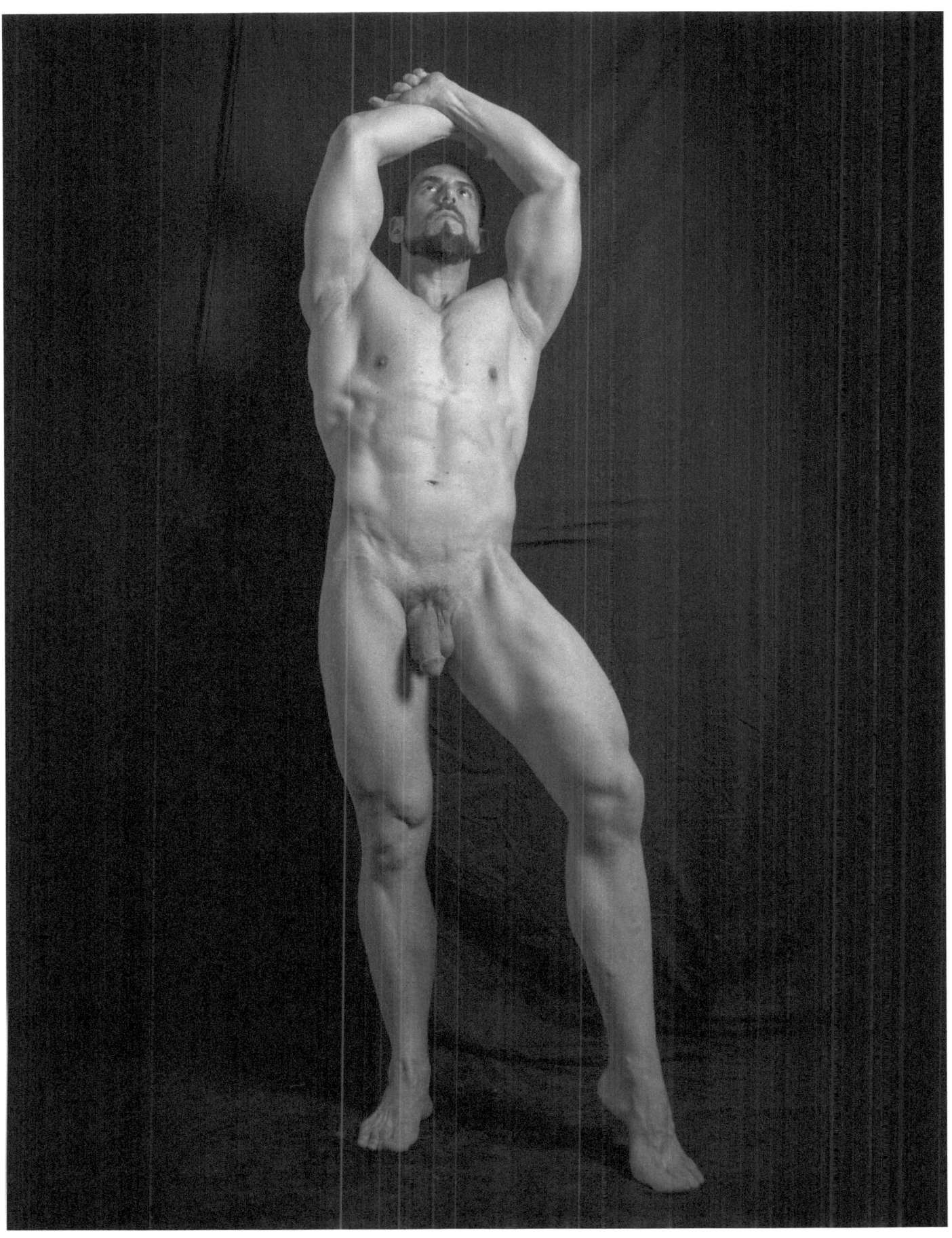

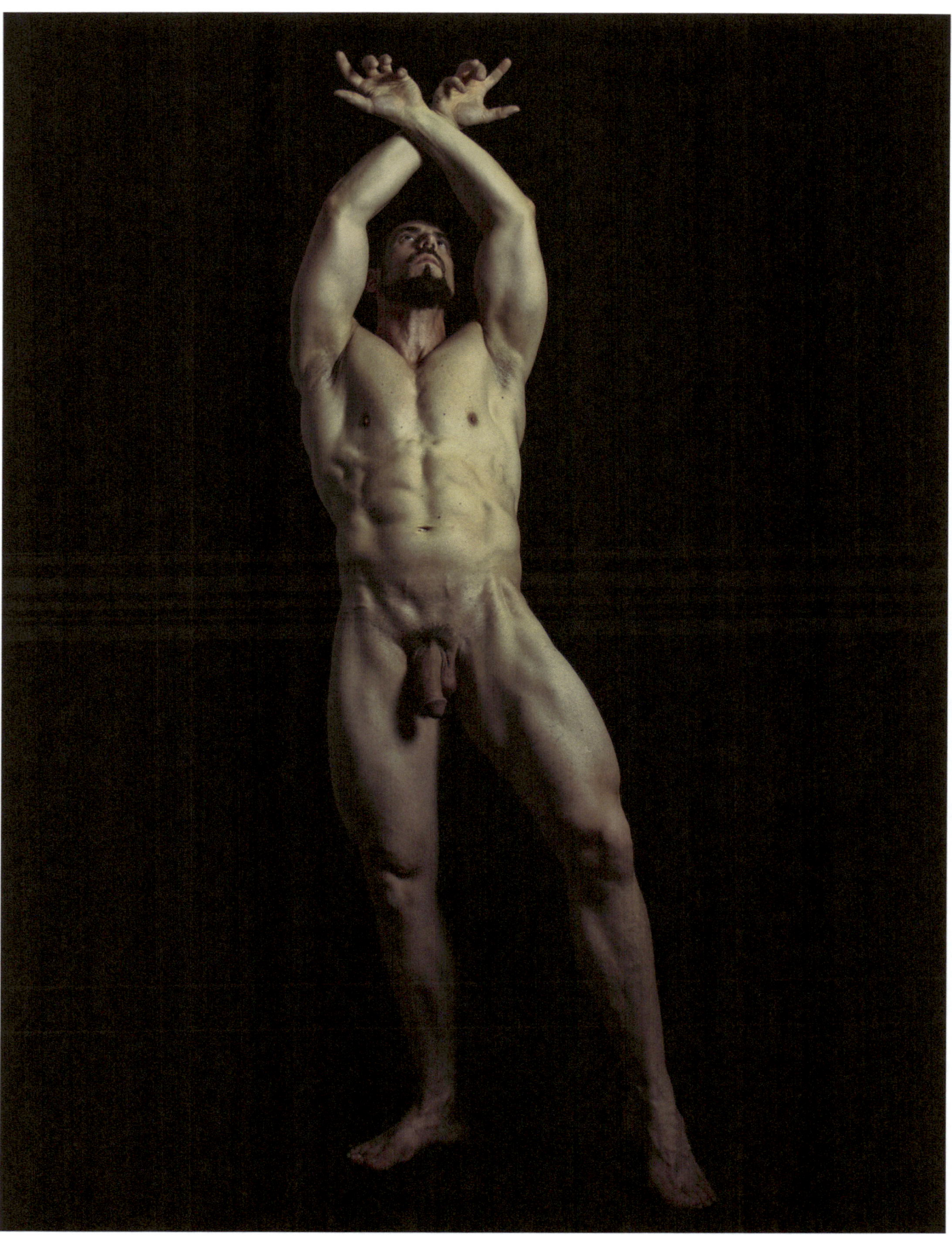

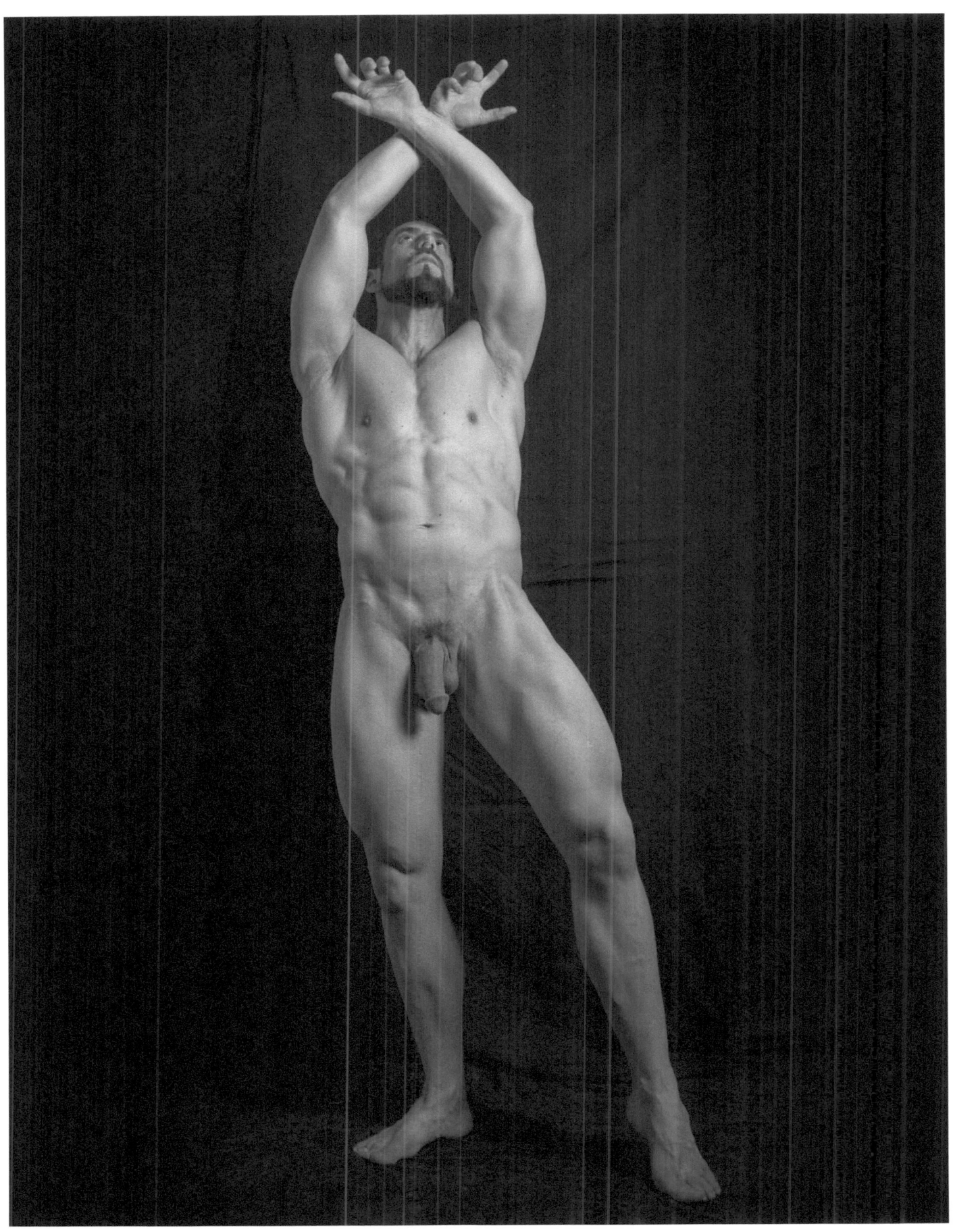

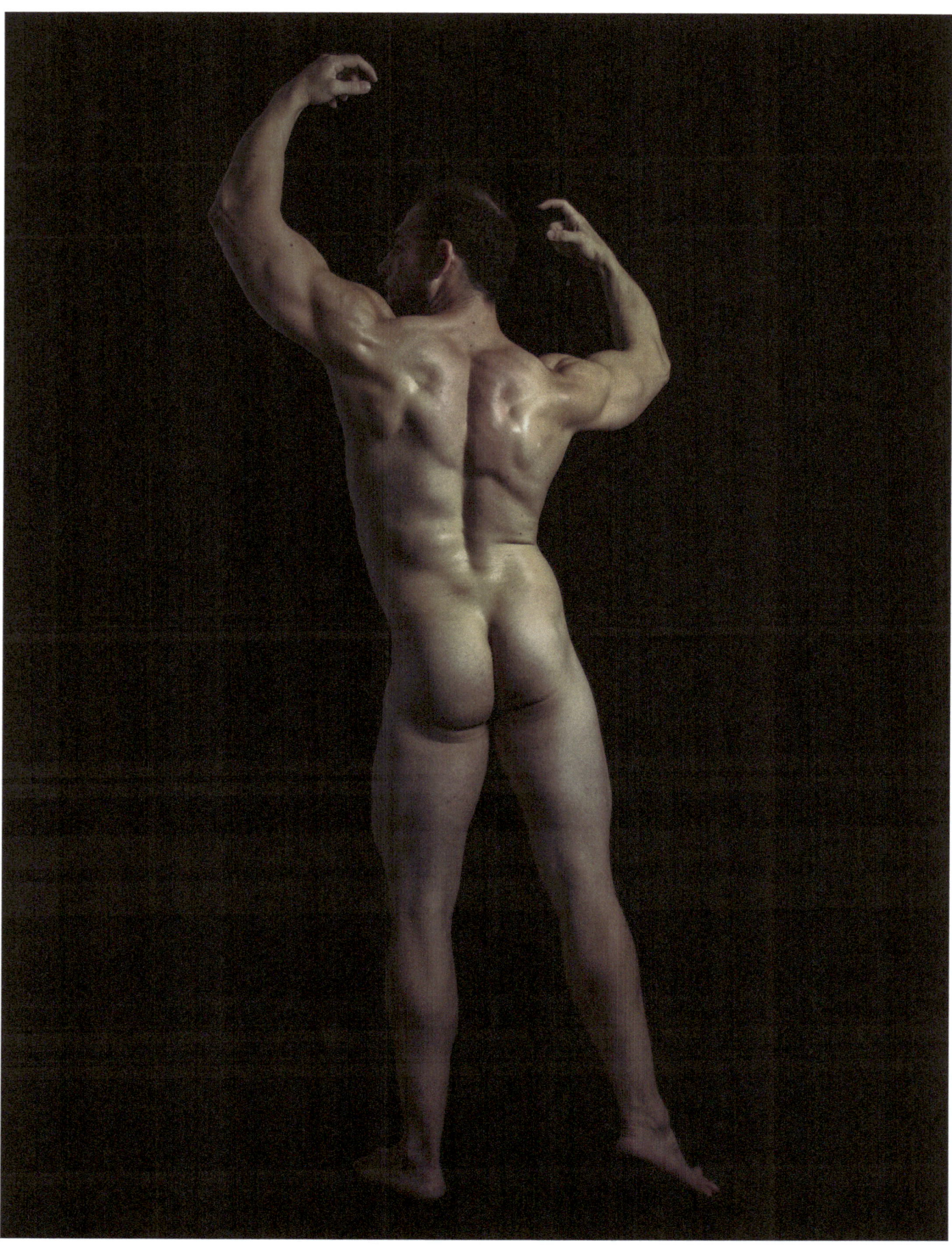

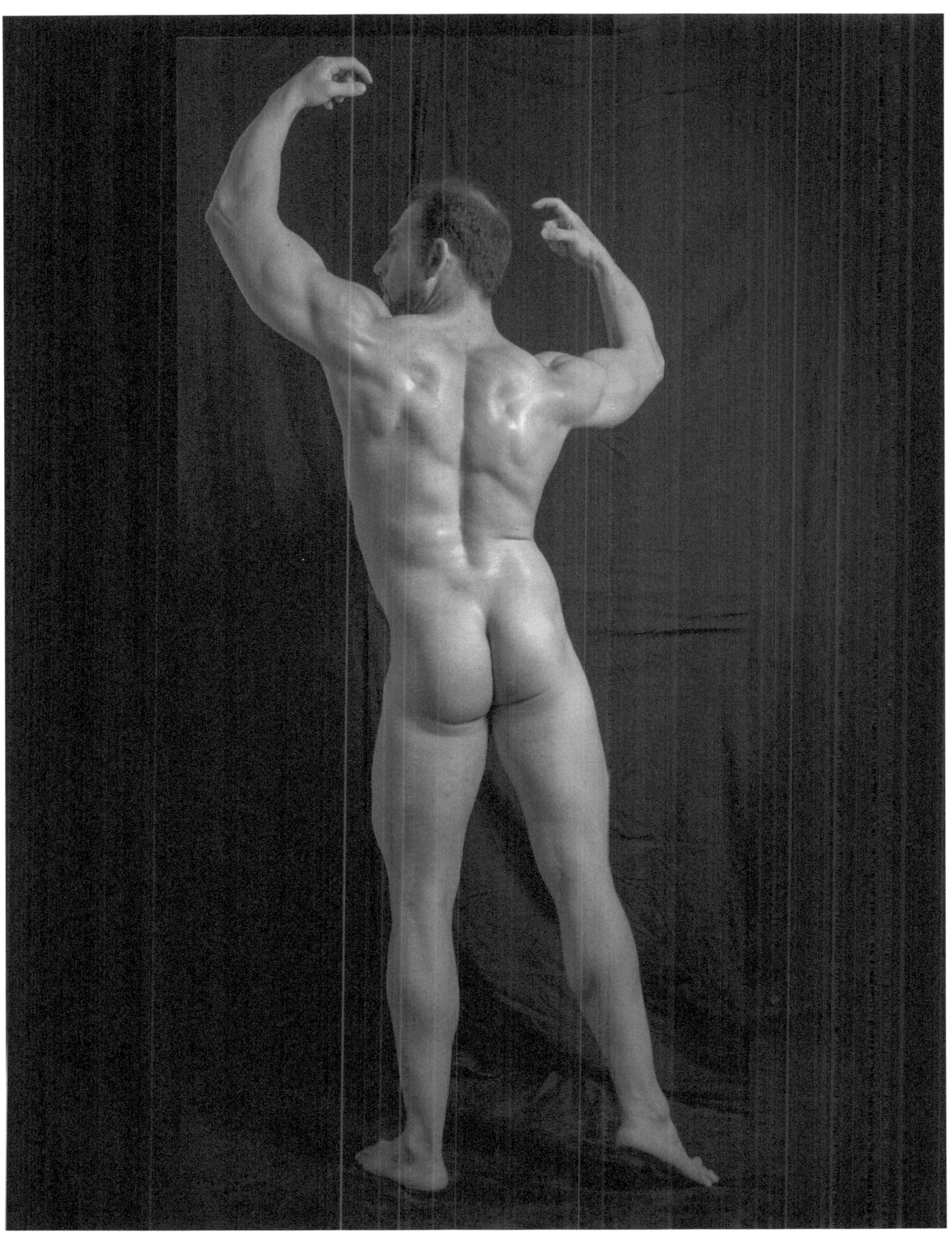

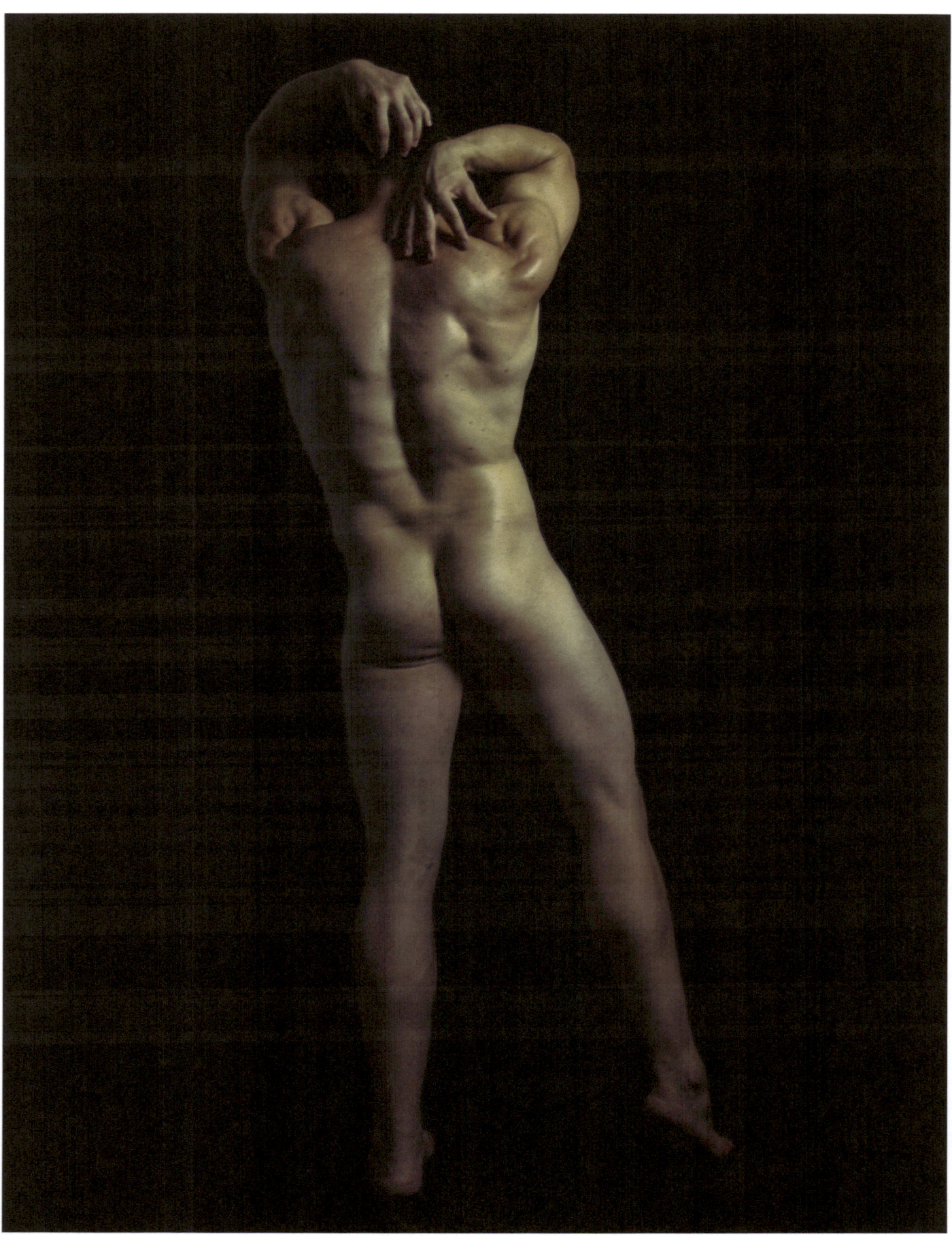

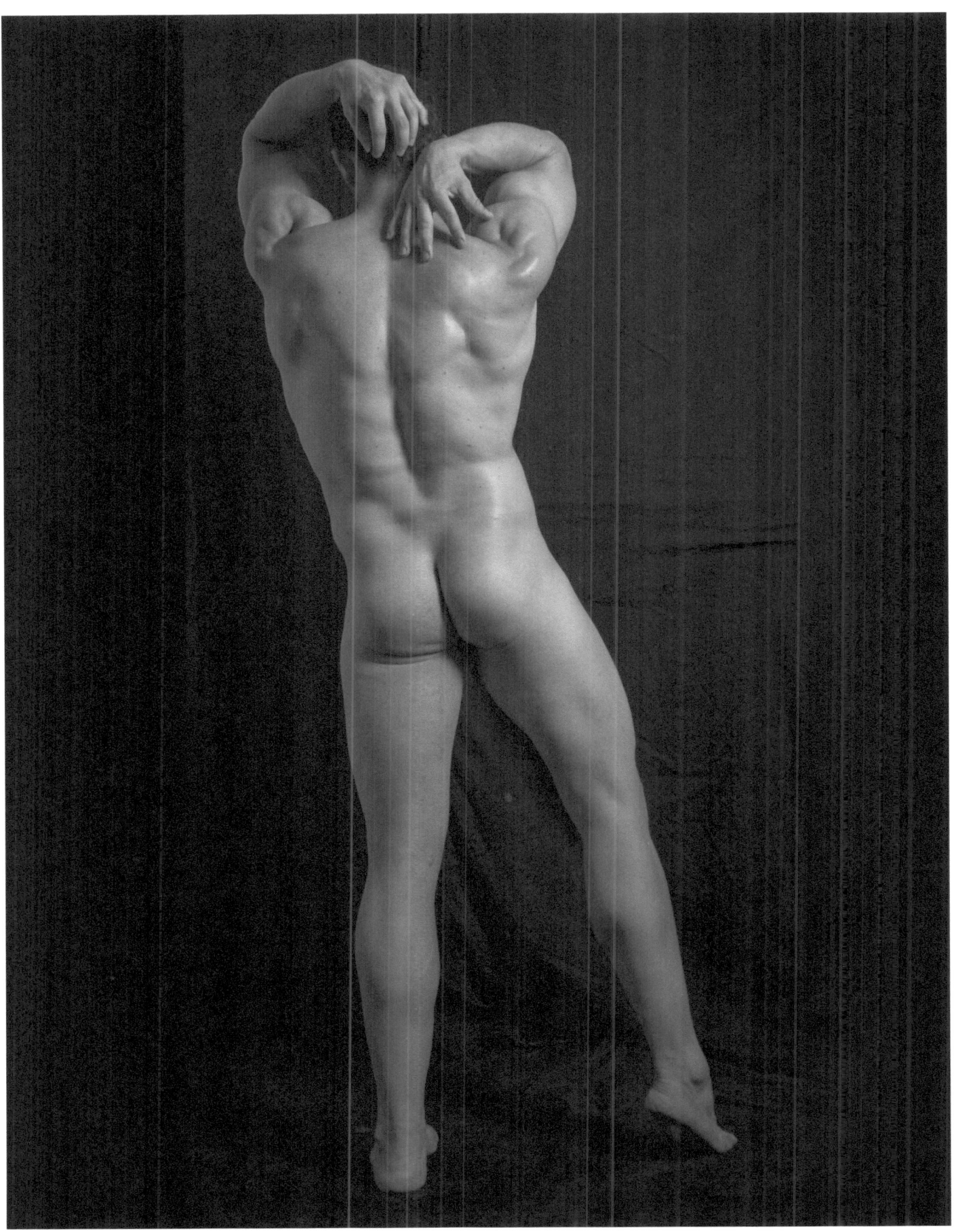

LOOK FOR MORE POSE PHOTO SERIES
FEATURING YONI BAKER-

COMING SOON!

www.ingramcontent.com/pod-product-compliance
Lightning Source LLC
Chambersburg PA
CBHW040409220526

45473CB00004B/1181